LIGHT ON PROPHECY

LIGHT ON PROPHECY

Retrieving Word and Spirit in Today's Church

Jennifer Campbell

Paternoster:
thinking faith

18 17 16 15 14 13 12   7 6 5 4 3 2 1

This edition first published 2012 by Paternoster
Paternoster is an imprint of Authentic Media Limited
52 Presley Way Crownhill, Milton Keynes, MK8 0ES
www.authenticmedia.co.uk

British Library Cataloguing in Publication Data

A catalogue record for this book is available from the
British Library.

ISBN 978-1-84227-768-3

Cover design by Paul Airy at DesignLeft (www.designleft.co.uk)

For my father Peter Campbell 1928–2005

Abbreviations

Abbreviations used in endnotes:

AB Act and Being
CCCM Corpus Christianorum: continuatio mediaevalis
CF Creation and Fall
D Discipleship
E Ethics
EP Hildegard Bingensis Epistolarium
GS Gesammelte Schriften
LDO Hildegard Bingensis Liber Diuinorum Operum
LHB The Letters of Hildegard of Bingen
LPP Letters and Papers from Prison
LT Life Together
LVM Hildegard Bingensis Liber Vite Meritorum
MW Meditating on the Word
NRS No Rusty Swords
PB Prayerbook of the Bible
SC Hildegard Bingensis Scivias
SC Sanctorum Communio
SYM Symphonia Armonie Celestium Revelationum
VH Vita Sanctae Hildegardis
WF The Way to Freedom
YB The Young Bonhoeffer

CONTENTS

Abbreviations   vii
Preface   xi
Foreword   xv
Introduction   xvii
    The Biblical View   xviii
    The Problem Today   xx
    Hildegard and Bonhoeffer   xxv

1 Crucible of Vision   1
    Hildegard of Bingen: Voice of the Living Light   3
    Dietrich Bonhoeffer: Voice of One Man   15
    One Life   29

2 Scripture and Vision   31
    Limitations of the Historical-Critical Method   32
    Retrieval of Patristic-Medieval Exegesis   33
    Hildegard of Bingen: Recovering the Prophetical
      Way in Scripture   34
    Dietrich Bonhoeffer: Reviving the Spiritual Meaning
      in Scripture   49
    Reading the Signs of the Times through Scripture   59

3 Community of Vision   61
    The Social Network   61
    The Person of Jesus Christ   65
    Hildegard of Bingen: Cosmic Community of Light   66
    Dietrich Bonhoeffer: Community of the Cross   78
    Verus Homo/Verus Deus   88

4   Visionary Dreamers   90
        Spiritual Cataracts   91
        The Person of the Holy Spirit   92
        Hildegard of Bingen: Supernatural *Visio*   95
        Dietrich Bonhoeffer: Creative Speculation   106
        Faces Unveiled   116

    Conclusion   118
    Bibliography   124
    Endnotes   134

Preface

> I ask not only on behalf of these, but also on behalf of those who will believe in me through their word, that they may be one. As you, Father, are in me and I am in you, may they also be in us, so that the world may believe that you have sent me (Jn. 17:20–21)

The night of the betrayal and arrest of Jesus Christ, known as Maundy Thursday, is marked by the great prayer for unity on the lips of the Lord. As the Trinity is inseparable so must the church be unified for the greater purpose of winning the world. Jesus shows this unity with his Father's will as he humbly surrenders to the agony of the cross. On Good Friday his shout of victory, 'It is finished', is a cry of triumph that his broken body will be the instrument for piecing together the fragmentation of the people of God for all time. His robe at the foot of the cross is seamless. Christ desires our oneness and he died for it. On Holy Saturday the death of God in the stillness of the grave and the interval of utter silence represents the Body of Christ entombed as she awaits the quickening breath of the Spirit. And on Easter Day a universal shout of victory ascends to the vault of heaven: 'Christ is risen! He is risen indeed! Alleluia!' In a unified acclamation the worldwide church drops her guard, her lesser denominational defences, for the greater witness.

However, in order to fan this unity into reality, we must give vent to another shout, 'Come Holy Spirit!' as we pray toward Pentecost for a fresh breath, for a live coal on the mouth of the church to burn and scorch with the living Word. If the testimony of Jesus really *is* the Spirit of prophecy (Rev. 19:10d) then we ought to *be* a prophetic people with less division and more witness to the incredible saving grace of God. The church will remain in its grave-clothes of mediocrity, dullness and strife, the world will continue to disregard us – even to hold us in contempt – unless a united, purified people arises as a prophetic change-agent to challenge, provoke and inspire.

What is a unified prophetic testimony to Jesus? This book is an apologia for a retrieval of robust prophecy which flows strongly at the confluence of the mighty streams of church tradition: sacramental, evangelical, Pentecostal, charismatic, social gospel, pietistic. It is a plea to embrace the entire spectrum, to gather up denominational fragments and to hold fast our unity in the Spirit so that Christ may be glorified and the world may believe. The truth is, however, that at all levels – local, national or international – we grapple with issues of unifying churches whose doctrines accentuate the Word with those who hold out for the full measure of the gifts of the Spirit. The prophecy for Great Britain by the revivalist, Smith Wigglesworth (1859–1947), is both a yardstick for reflection and an incentive for mission:

> [T]here will be evidenced in the churches something that has not been seen before – *a coming together of those with an emphasis on the Word and those with an emphasis on the Spirit* [italics mine]. When the Word and the Spirit come together, there will be the biggest movement of the Holy Spirit that the nation, and indeed the world, has ever seen . . . The outpouring of God's Spirit will flow over from the United Kingdom to the mainland of Europe, and from there will begin a missionary movement to the ends of the earth.[1]

My thanks are due to those who have believed in this project: Dr Philip Meadows, former colleague in the postgraduate department at Cliff College, who strenuously upheld the main thesis of the book; Professor Kathleen Coleman, who not only hosted me at Harvard University for eight weeks, but painstakingly read and edited portions of the draft material; Dr Mike Parsons of Paternoster who continued to be unsurprised at my offerings; Mollie Barker, copy-editor, who suggested helpful and useful amendments; many praying friends in South Africa and England, especially my mother, Stella, who believed in me and strengthened my resolve to write. Finally, I am hugely indebted to the north Wiltshire community among whom I live and share my life, for their unwavering support. Nevertheless, despite all practical and spiritual assistance, any matters of infelicitous style, inconsistencies or errors are mine alone.

Jennifer Campbell
Oxford
Easter Day, 2011

Foreword

Jennifer Campbell's book is about the role of prophecy in the modern church. She bases her vision of this role on the spiritual writings of two German theologians who are not usually examined together: the medieval mystic, Hildegard of Bingen, who founded convents and engaged bishops in theological debate; and the twentieth-century Lutheran pastor, Dietrich Bonhoeffer, who was executed days before the end of World War II for his involvement in a plan to assassinate Adolf Hitler.

To many of us, Hildegard of Bingen is no more than a name. That name is evidently female and evidently borne by someone long ago, judging from the fact that her place of domicile, Bingen am Rhein, takes the place of a surname; so one feels vaguely surprised that a woman could have written so influentially in the Middle Ages as still to be read today. Dietrich Bonhoeffer is perhaps a little more familiar, but maybe better known for his resistance to Hitler than for his theology. And, as for prophecy, what is that? The sort of thing for which Nostradamus is ridiculed? Spotting the Second Coming? Being able to predict the stock market? The average churchgoer looking for stimulating reading might well be both intrigued and a little wary.

But Jennifer Campbell's book makes sense. The devotional Hildegard and pragmatic Bonhoeffer each speak to a twenty-first-century audience, though in different ways. And prophecy turns out to be the recognition of Christ at work in the contemporary world – a recognition not easy to achieve, given the 'noise' and distraction of our predominantly secular concerns. Ms. Campbell argues that that state of recognition and conviction of Christ's place in the world, and our obligation to identify what he needs us to do, is to be achieved by the union of Word and Spirit. This union is exemplified, respectively, in the writings of two fellow countrymen almost a millennium apart, who spoke with a distinctly individual voice in their own day.

Bonhoeffer and, especially, Hildegard are not easy to understand. Jennifer Campbell sets their work in its historical context, and unpacks their prophetic vision – Hildegard's emphasis on the Holy Spirit as the conduit of divine revelation, and Bonhoeffer's placing of Christ in the centre of everything. At every stage she quotes from their work, in English translation, and traces the scriptural passages that inspired them. In the course of her exposition she outlines some of the relevant developments in modern theological scholarship, but her learning is worn lightly; it is possible to understand what she is saying without recourse to the works cited in the endnotes, although the references are there for those who want to pursue them.

Jennifer Campbell faces the hard questions: how to distinguish a true prophet from a charlatan; how to combine desire for God with the responsibilities of living in the world as it is today; how to interpret Scripture both faithfully and imaginatively; how to reconcile the voice of the individual prophet with the communal voice of the church; and much else. She resists the temptation of reducing the beauty of Hildegard's imagery to conform to prosaic interpretation. She is brave enough to quote passages from Bonhoeffer that seem to 'secularize' Christianity in an attempt to match the message of the Scriptures to the needs of contemporary audiences.

This is a provocative book. It brings two different worlds to life – one the hazy world of a cloistered medieval nun, the other the horrific moment when the energy of the Weimar Republic gave way to the ideology of the Third Reich – and shows that its chosen representatives of those two very different times are able to deliver a message of challenge and hope to the ordinary men and women of the twenty-first century who sense a need for renewal in the Christian message and in the parishes that are its crucible.

Kathleen M. Coleman
James Loeb Professor of the Classics
Harvard University
September 5, 2011

INTRODUCTION

> Therefore every scribe who has been trained for the kingdom of
> heaven is like the master of a household who brings out of his
> treasure what is new and what is old (Matt. 13:52).

This work is born of an innate curiosity and fascination with
God-talk. Does God talk to us? If so, how do we hear and see him,
and what is he saying? The noisy cacophony of opinion-makers
in the global village network appeals to any kind of wisdom or
enlightenment for the resolution of problems in the international
arenas of politics, economics, ideologies, philosophies, science
and religion. These ideas ought to challenge church leadership: Is
this really God? If not, then what *is* the word of the Lord for
nations, governments, institutions, the academy, the media, the
community, local church, my family? Where is it to be found?
And most importantly, is the word of the Christian God legitimate in multinational, multicultural, multi-religious contexts?
Christians who lead in both sacred and secular spheres seek a
godly viewpoint. In ministry situations pastors, teachers, evan-
gelists, apostles or missionaries deal with the complexity of the
human problem. In the workplace business associates, educators,
politicians or financiers must be forward-thinking and plan
strategically.

At the interface of the word of the Lord and the concrete situation stands the prophet. The prophet lives to hear a different
note which comes from the future and is played in the present
reality. The forerunner goes ahead to hearken to the higher sound
and to bring back from the future a song for the present. In its
general biblical use the word 'prophecy' means the spoken word

as it comes in inspired utterance, in prediction, in the public interpretation of Scripture or in preaching, as the direct communication from God, that is, as the 'word of the Lord'. Intrinsic to the
term is the biblical understanding of prophecy's generation in
non-verbal ways, that is, through vision, dream, sign or action.
Likewise, the word 'prophet' means a messenger of deity, an
inspired teacher or preacher who speaks in the name of God.

This book is an incomplete investigation of the thorny issue of
Christian prophecy. It is not a manual on how to use the gift of
prophecy, but it points a way for further thinking into some of its
many complexities as it grapples with the contentious sticking
points of authority, sources of divine wisdom, Scripture, the seer,
the supernatural, dreams and visions. It seeks to address these
problems by means of a theological excavation of the past, to dig
up treasures to resource the present, from the vast spiritual
wealth within the two-thousand-year tradition of the universal
church. The theological movement of *ressourcement* (return to
source) promotes a whole new vision to revive and revitalize pri-
orities for our critical times.[1] To this end I have chosen two visionaries 800 years apart who spoke for Jesus Christ and exemplify
the prophetic lifestyle: the medieval German Catholic Hildegard
of Bingen (1098–1179) and the modern German Lutheran Dietrich
Bonhoeffer (1906–45). These two persons have large minds and
spirits open to God and to the world to fathom the depths of the
human condition and the divine mercy. Their cocked ears are
attuned to God's voice for their generation although the notes
they hear, and sound, are from two distinct scores. Hildegard is
an enclosed monastic and her vision comes from the presence of
the supernatural Living Light; Bonhoeffer is a pastor theologian
and his vision is achieved in a political matrix in the hurly-burly
of a climate of war. I have put their works under a microscope in
order to enlarge the specific contribution each offers to the scope
of prophecy in its broad sense.

The Biblical View

The question of Christian prophecy for multiple scenarios close
at hand or further afield is related to the sovereignty and lordship

of God over the earth. If the voice of God is to be heard in the world today it is permissible to expect that the prophet, as well as the church as prophetic voice, has something God-ordained to say and to do in sacred and secular settings. This understanding is in harmony with the New Testament, which is concerned with prophetic leadership given either by individuals or by the church as a whole. That pattern is established in the Old Testament, where Israel itself is a prophetic people, and sages or leaders are God-appointed as oracles of divine intelligence with the spirit of wisdom or rational sense. The Bible has two views on the times as known and unknown to human beings.

The Chronicler is optimistic about the 'knowability' of the times. The tribe of Issachar has the responsibility to bear the specific vision for Israel: 'Of Issachar, those who had understanding of the times, to know what Israel ought to do' (1 Chr. 12:32). Forecasters in sacred spots tell Israel what to do: 'They used to say in the old days, "Let them inquire at Abel"; and so they would settle a matter' (2 Sam. 20:18). Then there is the appeal to the wise man to settle Persian state affairs in Esther 1:13: 'Then the king consulted the sages who knew the laws (for this was the king's procedure towards all who were versed in law and custom)'.

The Preacher, however, is pessimistic about the unknowable God. The book of Ecclesiastes resonates with the theme that wisdom is an attribute of God that corresponds to the times (3:1–8). However, the times cannot be predicted and lie outside of human control (3:9–15). When God judges (3:17; 11:9), human beings cannot make sense of these divine judgements, or indeed of anything which God does. The writer is emphatic: 'moreover, he has put a sense of past and future into their minds, yet they cannot find out what God has done from the beginning to the end' (3:11). There is an underlying futility in the search for wisdom: 'However much they may toil in seeking, they will not find it out; even though those who are wise claim to know, they cannot find it out' (8:17, cf. 11:5).[2]

Thus a tension is brought to bear on prophecy as the inscrutable mysterious God and the curious enquirer co-exist in a creative partnership. In this co-operative, human reason respects God's higher intelligence, and inactive passivity, which determines to do and to say nothing on the grounds of God's sovereignty, is challenged with responsibility.

The Problem Today

To review the situation of prophecy in the contemporary church is to sketch a bleak landscape. The sound of thunder in the ancient prophetic voices is a whisper in the twenty-first century, so still and small as hardly to be heard at all. Turbulent world events charge the spiritual atmosphere, and gathering clouds on the windswept plains of spirituality hold the promise of the rain of God's word on dry land. But when the heavens are as brass, prophets bang their drum and march to the sound of their own voice. The vacuum in the public domain is filled with the sounds of eccentricity. Self-appointed street preachers proclaiming the exact date of the end of the world amuse and anger us. Self-proclaimed gurus advertising healing on every airwave lure us. We are sceptical about rumours of apocalyptic disasters posted on websites and blogs, or post-apocalyptic panoramas in film. Untouched we walk by signs of the times written on subway walls and drive under bridges announcing Jesus. This sort of random prophecy outside the boundaries of church leaves us unfazed and sceptical, and within the wider church prophecy is a minefield. The catastrophe of the Nine O'Clock Service in Sheffield, England, in the early 1990s, is a chilling reminder of self-important prophets wreaking havoc outside close-knit accountability structures. The exposé of malpractice within the Kansas City prophets in the 1990s alerts us to the dangers of misguided spiritual zeal.

The picture is little changed within the local church. In the mainline denominations we are disturbed at anything too supernatural or out of the ordinary. We quail at the thought, never mind the practice, of emotional outbreaks interrupting and disturbing the peace, the pace and rhythm of our services. And in charismatic or community churches the gift of prophecy is reined in, harnessed and managed so as to follow the leader and not veer off track. We are delighted that fervent exhibitions of love for God and accompanying spiritual gifts find a place in

Pentecostal, Afro-American or Latin American gatherings, in Toronto-style conventions and the like, but for day-to-day living and working, it is business as usual. Messy church once in a while, helped by the presence of children; spiritual gifts monitored; prophetic people kept in check and in step with leadership. In this way congregational anxieties are minimized, leadership harmony is maximized and the drought of the word of the Lord remains unbroken. However, if spiritual famine is to be alleviated and the hungry fed, then, disturbing as its presence and practice may be for ordinary church members, uncomfortable as its challenge may appear for practitioners and leaders, it is imperative that the gift of prophecy be set free to come out of the closet as an authentic, life-giving part of church tradition and practice. In theory the recovery of the ministry of prophecy is desirable. In practice it is likely to be an awkward and prickly bedfellow. A plethora of objections rush to the aid of leaders reluctant to engage at any depth with prophetic people.

Intellectual annihilation

One objection is the worry of prophetic excess or extremes. If the credibility of the Western church is to be sustained in its struggle to stay alive in secular society and to maintain its shelf life in a supermarket of faith options, then mental suicide is not the way forward. Christians are noted, not only for their steadfastness down the centuries, but for rebellious actions against powerful regimes of church and state. If one or two crazy prophetic types want to shave their heads or grow their beards or dwell in trees as signs of contradiction to the spirit of the age, so be it; there is nothing to stop them. However, protest is not the call of all and certainly not everyone's cup of tea. Heaven forbid that a rash of banner-waving, placard-holding, strident speech-making infect the body corporate. The word of the Lord must certainly go out, but in church, quietly and with orderly discretion, not shouted loudly or bodily in the public square or national television or Radio 4. Religion is a private matter and has nothing to do with the state or the common good. Martyrdom is given and not sought. It is far wiser and safer to sail close to the wind within mainstream middle-way faith, than to set a course into the unknown wilds of the unpredictable prophetic community.

History is littered with the fanatical fringe which has wounded the witness of the church.

Much prophetic activity seems to be generated by emotion; for example, shaking, shouting, dancing, drumming, rhythmic movement, swaying, voices, ecstatic song and tongue speaking. Moreover, these phenomena are indistinguishable from similar practices in witchcraft, the occult, the New Age, or drug-induced states. There is no objective means of testing these psychological manifestations, which are based on personal experience, or may arise from pathological disorders. The groundbreaking work of the American philosopher and psychologist William James (1842–1910) in the prestigious Gifford Lectures (1901–02), *The Varieties of Religious Experience*, elevates the subconscious or subliminal as the seat of religious mysticism, 'the fountainhead of much that feeds our religion', and delegates all non-rational impulses, passions, superstitions and convictions to its control. This is not good news for church leaders, especially as James concludes that, for those deeply into the religious life, 'the door into this region seems unusually wide open.' The rule of thumb – if it works for you it must be true – is simply not good enough for an assessment of Christian prophecy. On the centennial of James's death should we rejoice that his work celebrates the individual or despair that it legitimizes the crackpot?[3]

The sufficiency of Scripture

Another objection is grounded in the tension between prophecy and Scripture. The church already has the Bible as its guide and inspiration through which God has spoken for centuries. The Scriptures enunciate the high place the prophets occupied in antiquity to predict the Messiah, and with the coming of Jesus Christ the final word has been uttered. The era of the soothsayer is past: 'Long ago God spoke to our ancestors in many and various ways by the prophets, but in these last days he has spoken to us by a Son' (Heb. 1:1–2). The New Testament narrates the Christ event in a prophetical way and from now on the task of the church is to interpret that message. If the cessation of the dispensation of the gift of the prophet is a foregone conclusion, then from now on prophecies are superfluous and tricky. The tried and tested written word is the church's authority. The educated

Bible teacher is reliable; given free rein, the unlettered prophet may add or subtract from the Bible, or worse still, declare heresy. The egotistical prophet may diminish the importance of regular Bible study by a reduction into short sentences or piecemeal jargon a 'thought for the day'. Consistently serious and systematic reading of the Bible day by day to extract its wisdom is the way ahead; not the wacky oracle on Sunday.

The underworked Christ

There is also the objection to do with prophecy said to be deficient in christological content. If the 'testimony of Jesus is the Spirit of prophecy' (Rev. 19:10d) then all prophecy should point to his person. Clearly this does not seem to be the case at all in much prophesying. Instead there is an interest in dates and mates, in personal 'words' for people, in weather patterns and universal signs of cosmic upheaval. Rarely do we hear specific prophetic guidance about parish finance, for instance, and yet Jesus was interested in money. Visions from above suffer a lack of material substance from below and do not lead to anything really constructive. A contemplative who finds it easy to become lost in wonder, love and awe, and displays a shining face, is less likely to become lost in charitable works for neighbour and radiate the character of Christ. Staring at heaven above will not feed the poor, heal the sick, or bring about political change. When Jesus Christ prayed and taught his church to pray, 'Let your kingdom come on earth, as it is in heaven', he was instructing us in an ethic of pragmatism, asking us to attend to everyday detail, directing us to participate in life's temporalities and to find him in the faces of the grimy poor below, under the gaze and transforming power of heaven above.

The overworked Spirit

There is the objection over the questionable matter of prophecy and the Holy Spirit. The biblical principle that 'no prophecy ever came by human will, but men and women moved by the Holy Spirit spoke from God' (2 Pet. 1:21) gives licence to any dreamer to attribute quaking or shaking as a prophetic word from the Spirit, when it may just as well be the grumblings of a stomach subjected to a prolonged fast. Is the source of these rumblings truly the supernatural Third Person of the Trinity or will the prophet be rumbled as a fake? Are the hours spent in prayer, in fasting or ascetic rituals, in solitary ponderings away from the madding crowd not a devilish diversion from the real mission of the church? One has to question whether the absorption with an otherworldly reality 'out there' or a fixation with heaven and angels are healthy pursuits when our feet ought to be planted firmly in this world and its troubles. Surely dreams and visions are the stuff of fanciful imaginings of a pre-scientific bygone age and not from the Holy Spirit, who is also rather insubstantial and hard to imagine. The work of the Spirit is to lead us to a sane, rational and ethical life, not to live as though we already inhabit the afterlife. The conclusion reached in a recent study of the evolution of religion by an anthropologist, Lewis-Williams, is that today many accept that there are no such things as mystical beings and supernatural realms. We may enjoy the aesthetic experience of the Last Judgement in the Sistine Chapel, or wonder at the stars, without being religious or believing in God's supernatural intervention. You can be a 'thoroughly decent person without God breathing down your neck'.[4]

* * *

This analysis is by no means exhaustive, but it is a springboard into the deep and murky waters of prophecy, in order to draw up four cardinal points to frame the discussion in four successive chapters:

1. The life of the prophet as the crucible of vision
2. The revival of the spiritually prophetic sense in Scripture
3. The testimony of Jesus Christ cosmic and crucified
4. The prophetic Holy Spirit

Each area is tackled with reference to the life and works of Hildegard of Bingen and Dietrich Bonhoeffer and a way forward is suggested which overcomes the negatives and moves the arguments about prophecy towards a positive and creative resolution. In each chapter there is an emphasis on the work of Christ and the function of the Holy Spirit and the strength or weakness of each divine person dependent on the particular theological viewpoint of Hildegard and Bonhoeffer, in relation to the topic under discussion.

Hildegard and Bonhoeffer

Chapter 1 investigates the crucible which produced the Hildegard phenomenon: a mystic guided by the Living Light with the handrails of the Benedictine Rule and Scripture to prevent doctrinal error; an uneducated woman with access to some scholarly material, in contact with leading intellectuals; an outspoken critic of male and female leaders in church and state, constantly in the public eye. Her mysticism is elite and not easily accessible. Her vision is unasked for and comes from outside herself. In this respect she passes Bonhoeffer's test for true religious experience. In a book review of *The Varieties of Religious Experience*, Bonhoeffer critiques James's view of the subconscious because it misses the transcendental aspect. Religious experience which comes from the subconscious is illusory. It must come from 'really outside', from God, and not from within the human being.[5] Paul's Damascus illumination (Acts 9:1–9), for example, plainly illustrates this foundational point. Bonhoeffer's crucible is the turmoil of Germany between two world wars. His theological vision is led by questions of the day and is punctuated by divine insights which clarify and set him in opposition to colleagues in church and university academy, and ultimately with the Third Reich itself. He keeps in step with the fast pace of changeable political moods and philosophical trends so that his theological scheme is not a well-built structured edifice but may be described as 'a deliberate non-system-building rationale that is marked by an inner sense of the dramatic instead of the static'.[6] Bonhoeffer is always on the move, an activist and a political animal, strenuously involved in acts of justice and kindness. At the end of the first decade of the twenty-first century, the passive model of 'faithful presence' in society, articulated by a Christian sociologist, Hunter, is not quite close enough to Bonhoeffer's prophetic witness in the first half of the twentieth century. The view that the task of the church is to 'decouple the "public" from the "political"' is a far cry from Bonhoeffer's stance.[7] Hildegard's

engagement with the supernatural sphere underlines the gover-
nance of the person of the Holy Spirit in the ordering of the
prophetic charism or gift. Bonhoeffer's task is always to pinpoint
the exact way in which the person of Christ effects the changes in
his theological vision. The cohesion of these two theological
visions opens a double door upon a wide and limitless horizon in
the exercise of prophetic speech.

Chapter 2 is a challenge to the separation of prophecy and the
Bible and an argument for their convergence, in order to recover
the prophetic sense within the text itself, by a recall of patristic-
medieval exegesis. This method of scriptural interpretation was
used by the early church fathers and dominated the way in which
the church critically examined texts up to the time of the
Reformation. Both Hildegard and Bonhoeffer demonstrate the
monastic discipline of meditation upon Scripture so that the higher, prophetical, pneumatic (spiritual) sense is gleaned from the
reading. Private and public situations are thus read in the stern
light of Scripture, and the word of the Lord is clearly spelt out for
that historic moment. The result of this exegetical method is a
dynamic up-to-date prophetic teaching, sermon or song. The use
of allegory, a deliberate surfeit of imagery, conveys with words
what is invisible and ethereal. It is a desire for more than meets the
eye, for what lies beyond appearances. The reliance of Hildegard
upon the prophetic Spirit for illumination of Scripture, in union
with the concentration of Bonhoeffer upon Christ as the centre of
Old and New Testaments, offers an holistic and spiritual reading
of the Bible.

Chapter 3 discusses the work of God accomplished by the
unity of the 'two hands' of God – Jesus Christ and the Holy Spirit
– and shows how the 'hand' of Jesus, or the 'testimony of Jesus'
as the 'Spirit of prophecy', is central to the visions of both
Hildegard and Bonhoeffer. Hildegard's vision of a flamboyant
cosmic community of the Trinity 'up there' is a painting in stark
relief to Bonhoeffer's suffering community of the cross, which
stands by God in his hour of grief 'down here'. A synthesis of
these two communities, which emphasize both heavenly and
earthly realities, is achieved by the person of Jesus Christ as the
interlocking component, both *verus Deus* (truly God) and *verus
homo* (truly man).

Chapter 4 pinpoints the necessity of the 'hand' of the prophetic Spirit in reclaiming the nearness of the supernatural and the dimension of visions and dreams. Hildegard's portrayal of the Spirit is elemental and life-giving but gives place at times to Mary as interlocutor and intermediary. Bonhoeffer stands at a juncture in the Lutheran tradition where the full weight of the pneumatology (the study of the person and work of the Holy Spirit) of the church fathers had been relinquished and replaced by the moral code of right behaviour. In his prison confinement he thinks again about the cross, and his barrenness is filled with creative philosophical speculation, in a dream of a renewed world on tiptoe, viewing a new horizon. The powerful portrait of the Spirit in Hildegard shows the weakness in Bonhoeffer's philosophical speculation. Her pneumatology is a plumb line for authentic and reliable prophetic utterance, especially that which purports to foresee future global landscapes and to predict the witness of the church therein.

The synergy of Christ and the Spirit at work in tandem – in the life of the prophet, in the reading of Scripture, in otherworldly or this-worldly realities, in dreams and visions – is an ingredient vital to a relevant prophetic remix for our contemporary church and world. By means of the principle of *ressourcement* in Hildegard and Bonhoeffer, there is a recovery of a robust presentation of both persons of Christ and Spirit in the traditions they represent, the marriage of which leads to life-giving prophecy.

1.

CRUCIBLE OF VISION

God, you have put us to the test,
refined us like silver,
let us fall into the net;
you have put a heavy strain on our backs,
let men ride over our heads;
but now the ordeal by fire and water is over,
you have led us out to breathe again
(Ps. 66:10–12, The New Jerusalem Bible).

The trouble with forerunners forging ahead with the word of the Lord in thought, word and deed is not so much the sound of the unfamiliar voice crying from the wilderness (unconventional and strange), or the apparent disregard for others in the Christian race (the flight of the alone to the Alone), but the utter conviction placed in the message they bear. This message is inextricably joined to the messenger, so that what is said cannot be divorced from what is seen, heard, felt and inwardly digested by the communicator. The prophet is a live flesh-and-blood witness who has seen the Lord, and that experience, that particular encounter, is an indelible and inerasable mark. Once having been grasped by God, the prophet is forever a testimony to Jesus Christ and alive in his hand. The extraordinary individual revelation of God may be unique and incomprehensible to most of us, but to *that* one, to the spokesperson to whom it is granted, the call is irresistible. The wider acceptance and reception of the one called is governed by the question, 'By what authority?' The response is confidence in the indefinable certitude that the Word which has laid hold will not let go until the purpose for which the message was

brought has been accomplished. And that word is not tameable,
but unfettered, risky, incalculably unpredictable.

The personal lives and writings of Hildegard and Bonhoeffer
are two sides of the same coin. They illustrate the necessity of the
working of prophecy as a gift of the Spirit (Hildegard) and the
revelation being totally in Jesus Christ and actualized in current
circumstances (Bonhoeffer). Hildegard and Bonhoeffer belong to
the category of prophetic voices from the edge, delivering a message in stark contrast to the accepted wisdom (or madness) of the
day. However, in their distinctive vocations, both point up the
paradox of genuine prophecy; that is, the dual duty to God *and*
church. In their appeals for the restoration of justice, their sever-
est critiques are reserved for the church whose servants they are.
The tension between individual and institution, between vision
and expediency, between the personal and the corporate is a
Catch-22 tightrope. Hildegard's stance cannot be labelled anti-
institutional; on the contrary, she allied herself with the institution in the service of orthodoxy. Her crusade, however, can be
termed a campaign ahead of its time; and herself a rebel in the
service of God's cause. Bonhoeffer's position can be called anti-
institutional in his identification with the Confessing Church and
its challenge to the Reich Church. His struggle for true and right
judgements, however, offered moral leadership to the whole
church on a broad scale.

Hildegard and Bonhoeffer are verbally outspoken in sermons
and letters, in the spoken or written word, but their theology is
by no means all protest. It is varied and reflects their distinctive
interests. The theological corpus of Hildegard is comprised of a
visionary trilogy, liturgical chants, songs, a morality play and
many other works on a variety of theological and philosophical
topics, including a book on natural sciences and medicine in two
parts. The theological works of Bonhoeffer comprise six books
published during his lifetime, one published posthumously, Bible
studies, catechetical works, journal articles, papers and reports;
his personal reflections are contained in poems, a play, letters and
papers from prison, diaries and a novel.

Hildegard of Bingen: Voice of the Living Light

> I will stand at my watch-post,
>> and station myself on the rampart;
> I will keep watch to see what he will say to me,
>> and what he will answer me concerning my complain (Hab. 2:1).

Hildegard was born into a family of high nobility and spent her early life in an agricultural region, on the Bermersheim estate near Alzey, Rheinhessen. At the age of 8 she was given as a 'tithe', from a family of ten children, to the monastery of Disibodenberg as one 'enclosed', under the supervision of the recluse Jutta von Spanheim, and at 16 she received the habit of a Benedictine nun. At 38 she was elected abbess of Disibodenberg and at 43 she began to record her visions. She wrote as a woman without a formal systematic education in Latin, although she received a monastic education with access to a library of biblical commentaries, was well versed in the patristic writings, and enjoyed intellectual exchange with friends, secretaries and mentors. Her copious correspondence was of two types, that initiated by herself and that instigated by others from far and wide. Her letter writers were drawn from ecclesiastical circles; for example, popes, Eugenius III, Anastasius IV, Hadrian IV; archbishops, Philip of Cologne, Conrad of Mainz; bishops, Eberhard of Bamberg, Daniel of Prague, Amalricus of Jerusalem; the Cardinal-Bishop of Tuscany, Odo of Soissons; Dean Philip and clerics of Cologne; abbots and monks, Bernard of Clairvaux; theologians, Odo of Paris. Her correspondents included crowned heads of Europe, emperors, Conrad III, Frederick I, Barbarossa; the Byzantine empress Irene; the English king Henry II, remembered for his clash with Thomas à Becket, and his wife, Eleanor of Aquitaine. Hildegard founded two convents at Rupertsberg and Eibingen, the former developing to the degree that its impressive buildings offered space for fifty nuns, staff and guests, all workshops being equipped with pipes for running water.

Awakening

Although Hildegard's noble upbringing, remarkable intellect and powerful friends contributed to her success as a sought-after church visionary in a wide field, her intrinsic authority as Sybil of the Rhine or Jewel of Bingen is derived from a higher source. Hildegard explains her dependency on God in a letter to Pope Eugenius III (d. 1153): 'It pleased this king to touch a small feather so that it flew miraculously, and a powerful wind sustained it so that it would not fall'.[1] The origin of her prophetic *visio* (vision) is in the supernatural order and implanted by God himself. There are many descriptions by Hildegard herself, as she tries to express the inexpressible, of the invasion of the numinous awakening her consciousness. In a reflection on her vocation, Hildegard likens her call from birth to the ancient Hebrew prophet, Isaiah (Isa. 49:1): 'When I was first fashioned, when in my mother's womb God raised me up with the breath of life, he impressed this vision in my soul'.[2] Hildegard is inwardly aware that she is both physically and spiritually conceived by the Lord. But on another occasion there is an external manifestation of God's presence. The hearing of an audible voice seals her conviction that the gift bestowed upon her from birth is spiritual and so foreign to her earthly nature that she may be assured of its divine authority. She writes, 'I heard a voice from heaven saying to me: "From infancy you have been taught, not bodily but spiritually"'.[3]

The pivotal moment of Hildegard's awakening as a prophet and a teacher comes in a super-sensory way, as a fiery physical sensation which suffuses her entire being in heavenly irradiation:

> When I was forty-two years and seven months old, the heavens opened, and a fiery light of the greatest brilliance came forth and suffused my whole brain and my whole breast with a flame. Yet it enkindled in a way that did not burn but warmed, just as the sun does when it warms anything on which it pours its rays. And suddenly I savoured the meaning and interpretation of books, that is, the Psalter, the Gospel, and other Catholic books of both the Old and New Testament.[4]

Mystical experiences form a starting block to launch Hildegard's undertaking to write down what she sees and hears. Divine illumination appears to be a constant companion throughout her life. In old age she writes of her captivation by the Living Light, that ecstatic perception which lifts her upwards into another plane so that she sees and hears what is ordinarily inaccessible to the human eye and ear. The Living Light, Hildegard's name for God, is subsumed within the circumference of a light of another kind, subtle and lustrous, which is called Shade of the Living Light and in whose brightness the visions are perceived. Within the Shade of the Living Light the visions become visible as fields of images, landscape, figures or forms:

> From my infancy until now, when I am in the seventieth year of my age, my soul has always beheld this Light, and in it my soul soars to the summit of the firmament and into a different air . . . The brightness which I see is not limited by space; it is more radiant than the luminous air round the sun and I cannot measure its height or its length or its breadth. Its name which has been given me is Shade of the Living Light, umbra viventis lucis . . . Within that brightness I sometimes see another Light for which the name Lux Vivens [Living Light] has been given me. When and how I see it I cannot tell, but sometimes when I see it, all pain and sadness are lifted from me and I seem a simple girl again and no longer an old woman.[5]

Others tell of Hildergard's extraordinary anointing. An unknown writer traces the origin of Hildegard's *visio* to a very early age: 'In her third year of age she saw so bright a light above her that she trembled in her entire being; but, being an infant, she was unable to convey anything about it'.[6] The monk Guibert of Gembloux (1124/5–1213) was a devotee and close confidant of Hildegard and he loves to follow her inspiration. In a letter to Bovo he describes her *visio* with poetic clarity:

> For these sources [Scivias and others] say that her soul was irradiated from her infancy with a certain light which she heard called the shadow of the living light, and that by means of it her soul ascended on high to the height of the vault in accord with the shifting patterns of the variable air and is spread over the various peoples however far away . . . she never suffers the unconsciousness of ecstasy, and that in describing the visions she uses no other words than those she has heard. She bears witness moreover that she was worthy of something even more amazing, which is that from time to time she sees in this light we have spoken of, another light,

which was named to her as the living Light. She is incapable of describing in words how she sees it . . . When did the world ever see and hear the like?[7]

Mystical prophet

It must be stated at the outset that the mystical way in Hildegard is not easily accessible to the majority. Her life as a mystic is fraught with great personal and physical distress. A very brief investigation shows the magnitude of stress she undergoes in the reception of her vision. In a letter to the university teacher Odo of Paris (d.1171), she testifies of her frailty: 'I, like the feather, am not endowed with great powers or human education, nor do I even have good health, but I rely wholly on God's help'.[8]

The arduous and uncertain character of Hildegard's illnesses gave rise in the modern period to theories of migraine which are now generally accepted. These assumptions are based on the claim that the flashing coloured lights, concentric circles, fortress figures, distortions of visual perception and sensory disturbances normally associated with the classic migraine can be applied to the reception of Hildegard's visions. There is the view that visual auras or 'scintillating scotomata', which are symptomatic of migraine sufferers, are the hallmark of the seer's experience and explain the nature of her visions. In an analysis of migraine Lewis-Williams advances the idea that the neural structure of the brain, in conjunction with deeply held beliefs, gives rise to periodic episodes of transcendence and momentary bliss. He postulates that Hildegard's visions are the product of mind-altering states, comparable to the rock art 'Illuminations' of the Stone Age San people of sub-Saharan Africa. He concludes that her writings could even have been a contrived means of gaining ecclesiastical support.[9]

For us today the migraine theory is an easy way of explaining and handling the oddities of mystics. It does not, however, take into consideration Hildegard's oeuvre: the sheer volume of material, the density and scope of the various scientific, medical, theological, musical and linguistic investigations, nor the sophisticated quality of her works. Is it possible that a corpus of such immense breadth, declared by her (and others) as the product of the Living Light, was the result *solely* of migraine? The time required for a literary output of such magnitude does not coincide with the comparative brevity of Hildegard's illnesses and her confinement to bed, physically and mentally incapacitated and unable to write. The migraine theory trivializes the entire mystical tradition that illness or compunction opens heaven and that physical manifestations are a sign of the coming of the Spirit of God. For example, Teresa of Avila (1515–82) writes of 'vehement impulses . . . as though my soul were being torn from me', and of the encounter with the angel whose spear 'seemed to pierce my heart several times so that it penetrated to my entrails'.[10]

Newman, a Hildegardian scholar, counters such theories of migraine. The Living Light is an 'internal mirror' for Hildegard's spiritual perception which is attuned to material reality. It never interferes with the normal working of her senses and comes and goes at will. The reception of the visionary light and the forms within it occur, firstly, in the stable condition of her being, followed, secondly, by the direct revelation from God. The effort of such 'double vision', the ordinary and the extraordinary at once, must have been an exhausting process. Her particular mode of seeing remains uniquely her own; even to her contemporaries it appears 'strange' and 'unheard-of'. The weightiness of Hildegard's call is a constant pressure. Her physical body becomes a battlefield. The phrase, 'great pressure of afflictions', is used to describe her bodily discomfort as well as the heaviness of the prophetic call and the trials she will face as the result of her own or others' resistance to the divine will. At defining moments of obedience to the heavenly vision, the words 'pressure of affliction' tellingly describe both physical pain and the frustration with those who do not share her vision.[11]

Authentication

We may argue that the reception and recording of such extraordinary occurrences is purely subjective and fallible as a result of human frailty. Nevertheless, as Hildegard the prophet moves through the allegorical landscape to interpret her experiences, there is a ring of authenticity in the writing. Three general tests for prophecy – communication, validation and prediction – are a gauge to measure Hildegard's *visio*.[12]

Communication

There must be a compelling sense of duty to communicate what has been received, with the result that prediction or inspired vision cannot be called prophecy until it is expressed. Hildegard's normal senses are never impaired or overcome to the degree that she is unable to communicate what she sees and hears. She is fully conscious and sees 'with wakeful eyes'. She writes of 'a vision seen not with my fleshly eyes but only in my spirit'.[13] She is an observer, aloof from the experience, distanced from the objects of her vision, almost as though the images are projected onto a screen, with little interaction with the figures. She writes: 'I do not see these things with my outward eyes or hear them with my outward ears or perceive them with the thoughts of my heart or through any contribution of the five senses, but only in my soul, for my outward eyes remain open, and I do not undergo the unconsciousness of ecstasy, but see them wide awake, by day and by night.'[14] Yet in her comprehension she is inspired by the Spirit. A recurring refrain is the phrase 'and I saw and I understood this'. It is often expanded to 'and I saw and understood this through the living Spirit'.[15]

Hildegard sees her visions within the Shade of the Living Light. She inhabits a dimension where she is neither in the world nor of it. An inner radiation passes through her conscious thought, and her entire being becomes a mirror, reflecting and transmitting divine messages. There is evidence to suggest that the transcribing of the communications may have taken place in the presence of another. The first Lucca miniature shows Hildegard receiving her fiery stream of inspiration in the company of Volmar (d.1173), who is her friend and scribe, seated and writing on parchment opposite her. This arrangement, together with the phrase 'she heard and by correcting discussed' in the 'Epilogue' of *Divine Works*, could imply that Volmar's assistance was synchronized to some extent with Hildegard's recording. Hildegard composed aloud and Volmar wrote at the same time, and at a later stage in discussion with her, sifted her words, so as to refine the Latin she had spoken.[16] It is difficult to categorize this composition as transcendental automatic writing; it has the stamp of human revision and refining. The message, however, must be from a transcendental source, i.e. God, and not from human invention – the second of the tests for authenticity.

Validation
Arguably the aspect of prophecy which most worries leadership is that of accountability and the relationship of the prophet to the church. Hildegard had friends in high places. The learned and influential abbot Bernard of Clairvaux (1090–1153) recognizes the charism (a gift given and anointed by the Holy Spirit) in Hildegard: 'When the learning and the anointing (which reveals all things to you) are within you, what advice could we possibly give?'[17] His patronage helps to persuade Eugenius III (d.1153) to give approval to her work. At the reading by the Pope of a copy of part of *Scivias* at the Synod of Trier (1147/48), the whole completed only in 1151, the assembled dignitaries judged that the visions and writings were from God and 'from the prophecy by which the prophets prophesied in times past'.[18] This key phrase approved the divine origin of the visions, comparable to the spirit of biblical prophecy. The validation of Hildegard's work is very significant, at a time when there is an acceleration of ecclesiastical interference in teaching or preaching of a suspicious nature. Hers is the first case on record of formal papal sanction of a potentially controversial theological work, a practice that would become increasingly common in the thirteenth century. Therefore in itself the work is a prophetic forerunner and a gateway to spiritual openness. The trend which begins to assert itself in the late eleventh century as 'evangelical enthusiasm' is the view that the gift of prophecy is a charism of the early church. Hildegard's legitimacy is conferred, therefore, by God and not by earthly authority.[19] It is interesting to note that, despite papal authentication and her dedication and fidelity to the church, Hildegard's canonization was uncertain, there being no official category for prophet-saints.[20]

Prediction
The final test, although not essential to prophecy, is the gift of prediction, probably the first thought which immediately springs to mind when prophets are mentioned. It may also be the characteristic of prophecy from which we most shy away, considering

it to be an untrustworthy, unreliable or fruitless pursuit. Prediction is the ability to look ahead into the future to tell those close at hand what is coming at a distance. Elisha the prophet, for example, tells the King of Israel the words that the King of Aram speaks in his bedchamber (2 Kgs 6:8–23). John of Salisbury (c.1115–1180) distrusts all occult forecasts but believes that prophesying the future is permitted, provided that one 'possesses the spirit of prophecy'. The underlying sense behind this phrase is that to be gifted in prophecy means that the foretelling is effective, with potency or strength, so that the prediction comes true (Deut. 18:22). John of Salisbury deliberately seeks out Hildegard's prophetic counsel for the outcome of certain political events. In 1167 he writes to Gerard Pucelle concerning the invasion of Italy by the emperor Frederick I, Barbarossa (1122/3–1190): 'I hold her [Hildegard] in commendation and reverence, since Pope Eugenius cherished her with an intimate bond of affection. Look carefully too and let me know whether anything was revealed to her at the end of this schism'.[21]

The biographical account, 'The Life of Hildegard', eagerly praises the seer's power to predict what is to come in great matters, but enthuses, too, on her gift to announce as revelation things absent to those present. Hildegard's gift of knowledge of things absent may have been slightly disturbing for those present with her in her religious communities, when 'at a time of silence, she would know about what and where, to whom and why, in what manner and for how long they were speaking'. Her ability to judge and discern human motives stands her in good stead as abbess: 'Because of the true prophetic spirit that was in her, she could *discern the thoughts* (cf. Lk. 5:22) and intentions of *human beings*, and so she rebuffed those who approached her in a perverse and frivolous cast of mind – as if to try her out'. She sees 'in spirit the past life and conduct of people, and in the case of some, she could even foresee the way their present life would end, and, according to the character of their conduct and merits, their soul's glory or punishment'.[22] It is vital that we understand that Hildegard's ability to predict and to communicate what she sees and hears is by virtue of the prophetic Spirit dwelling within her and it is that anointing which is perceived by church authority (see 1 John 2:26–27).

Profile of a visionary

Having examined closely Hildegard's call to be prophet and teacher, the stresses of that call and the acceptance by the wider church, it is important that we recognize her impact as a teaching, preaching prophet in her own day and in the present day.

Woman of the twelfth century

The twelfth century was no stranger to women visionaries; the authoritative visionary *magistra*, however, was unusual. The word *magister* (teacher) denotes not only one who teaches, but one with political power. There is no doubt that Hildegard is a heavyweight *magistra* (woman teacher) in her spheres of influence. Robert, abbot of Val Roi, is astonished that a woman should be such a source of inspiration in society to so many.[23] As *magistra* Hildegard is technically subject to male authority. As has been shown above, however, she has an acute awareness of her divine commission, and her first call, therefore, is to the *magisterium* (teaching, advice, instruction) of the Holy Spirit (Luke 12:12; John 14:26). In 'Sequence for the Holy Spirit', for example, she invokes the Spirit as 'teacher of those who know'.[24] She is detached from the Pauline prohibition, 'I permit no woman to teach or to have authority over a man; she is to keep silent' (1 Tim. 2:12), but attached to the role of women prophesying (Joel 2:28; Acts 2:17; 21:9). Her loyal right-hand assistant and friend, Guibert of Gembloux, stresses her obedience to the Spirit and to the whole (catholic) faith: 'her own experience has learnt from the heart in wisdom', so that, being mindful of the instruction, 'she obeys the Spirit and does not obstruct the apostle whom he sends', thereby 'conforming to the catholic faith in everything'.[25]

Although papal validation opened a door for Hildegard and gave her a wide audience, she is not dependent upon a bishop for the interpretation of her visions, as is the case, for instance, with the early twelfth-century visionary Herluca of Epfach (d.1127). On the contrary, bishops, kings and religious seek answers from *her*, as in the case of Eberhard, bishop of Bamberg (d.1170), who requires a rejoinder on metaphysics from Hildegard directly through the inspiration of the Holy Spirit and superior to abstract logic. She is in demand as a spiritual theologian to contest the dominant heretical views of Gilbert de la Porrée (d.1154). Odo, teacher at the University of Paris and opponent of Gilbert, initiates a conversation with Hildegard, seeking her resolution of a thorny dispute concerning the divinity of the Father: 'Would you please explain to us in a letter what you perceive in the heavens about this matter?'[26]

Medieval authors draw our attention to the problem of semantics in their discussion of women preachers. Religious discourse from a male voice is termed a sermon or homily but from an unauthorized female, heretic or lay person they resort to the use of verbs, 'to announce', 'to proclaim', 'to exhort', but never 'to preach'. Hildegard's *Gospel Homilies*, a collection of exegetical sermons and teachings on Scripture delivered to her Rupertsberg community, are unique testimony to a medieval woman's biblical instruction, within the liturgical cycle, to her nuns. In the matter of the Cathars, a widespread heretical sect of Oriental origin, gaining influence over poor and powerful alike, Hildegard is a pamphleteer, producing visionary treatises of denunciation and rebuke of clergy for their failure to anticipate the dangers of the heresy. She is also an authorized public preacher, as is seen in the request for her public sermon (1163) in Cologne about the Cathars. The mission tours at an advanced age, in which she preached with unchallenged authority to men and women, are unprecedented among orthodox medieval women.[27]

Not only does Hildegard's gifting equip her to order and manage her communities in addition to the demands of the influential people who sought her counsel, but by the power of the charism she delves into science and medicine. She continues the Benedictine practice of 500 years: *Book on the Subtleties of Different Kinds of Creatures* (1150–60) is a combination of natural science, medicine, ancient tradition and folk experience. The 'Life of Hildegard' states, 'Moved by the spirit of prophecy, she also composed certain books on the nature of man, the elements and the variety of created things, and how human beings might derive help from this knowledge, and many other secrets'.[28] The Renaissance humanist and bibliophile Trithemius (1462–1516) extols Hildegard's remarkable insights: 'In the medical books, she records with a subtle exposition the many wonders and secrets of nature in such a mystical sense, that only from the Holy Spirit could a woman know such things'.[29] Dronke, a medieval textual exponent, avers that in her own day only the Islamic philosopher and scientist Avicenna (980–1037) is in some way comparable to Hildegard, as ethics, medicine and mystical poetry are among the fields conquered by both of them.[30] Her musical liturgical forms are innovative: irregular lines in the longer hymns, the invention of a new tonality, the *decachord*, a break with the rules of the dominant Gregorian chant, and a distinct sequence form.[31]

Hildegard today

Although Hildegard of Bingen may not have been on church best-seller lists or on the bookshelves of academics, the rediscovery and translation of many of her writings during the last thirty years has thrilled and delighted New Age travellers and practitioners who have a fascination with cosmological worldviews, alternative medicine and cosmic or spiritual energies. Christians who are intrigued by creation spirituality, gender in God, or body/soul harmonies have adopted her as their guru. Hildegard's work is attractive to musicians, ecologists, mystics, poets, scientists, feminists and artists alike.

In the rush to enlist Hildegard in the services of emerging progressive thought there have been serious misconceptions, even mistranslations, of her work, by seekers who by their intentional support of certain kinds of theology or mysticism unintentionally suppress her orthodoxy. Creation-centred spirituality or cosmic Christ theology teaches that the 'Word made flesh' is the divine presence in nature itself, which might seem to agree with Hildegard's teaching that every ray of God is God and consequently every creature is a ray of God, a divine expression of God: 'I flame over the beauty of the fields and sparkle in the waters, and I burn in sun, moon and stars . . . Thus I, the fiery force, am hidden in them'. This view follows a similar trajectory to that of a contemporary New Age teaching programme, 'A Course in Miracles', in which Hildegard is used to support the concept that sin and death is unreal and illusory: 'I, the highest and fiery power, have kindled every spark of life, and I emit nothing that is deadly. I decide on all reality. Everything God has done was done by the Deity before the beginning of time in the divine present.' However, for Hildegard, all created things are subject to the service of the Creator, as they

are only 'the materials for the instruction of mankind, which he
comprehends by touching, kissing, and embracing, since they
serve him'.[32] In her denunciations of the heretical sect of the
Cathars, Hildegard's orthodox views on creation are upheld in the
face of their prevailing dualism. The Cathar theology of two distinct spheres, a kingdom of a good God and a kingdom of the creator of the visible, material and evil world, from which imprisoned
spirits need to be freed, is remote from Hildegard's thought. Her
doctrine retains the distinction between creation and Creator,
never blurring the boundaries between Christ and the cosmos.

The film *Vision – Aus dem Leben der Hildegard von Bingen* (original German title), released in 2009 with screenplay and direction
by Margarethe von Trotta, is a stirring presentation of a likeable,
very human seer and her multifaceted talents in herbal medicine,
musical production, physiology and building construction.[33]
Although the conflicts with church and state are faithfully narrated, the reasons given for the turmoil Hildegard creates are
misleading. The emphasis on powerful, attractive personality
smudges the actual *visio*, so that the film suffers from the absence
of a robust portrayal of the prophet's challenging words and the
way in which vision and words upset or maintained the status
quo to the degree they did.

The danger of co-opting Hildegard's writings for particular
causes, however noble or interesting, is that the essential charism
that she offers is overlooked in the stampede to mould her into an
image compatible with fashionable spirituality. Her curiosity and
intelligent investigation into the arts of music, medicine and cos-
mology, although quite exceptional, are really of secondary interest. The gift of the Living Light is given in the first instance, not
to massage a troubled age with a heavenly salve (although it can
be a healing balm), but to stir up and quicken souls to righteousness, truth and mercy. In the broad scheme of her contribution to
church and society, Hildegard's call is *prophetissa* (prophet) and
magistra (teacher). Her prophetic teaching, preaching, songs,
counsel and admonition are directed toward the awakening of
souls to God. She has not left us with a path to follow to union
with God. Her singular mystical experience is never a map for
others but a means of communicating her vision of the whole of
life, history and the universe as deeply touched by God. Unlike

the contemporary spiritual climate, with its dichotomy between good 'spirituality' and bad 'religion', i.e. the institution or the evil destructive hierarchy, Hildegard integrates spirituality into the whole of life and religion. It is all one package. She is a far-sighted visionary, in conversation with the thought of her age, and yet far above and beyond her troubled times. Self-indulgent and self-centred religion, or 'my spirituality', has no place in Hildegard. We should not think, however, that she is a 'cold fish' in her single-minded devotion to the pursuit of justice; her passion for God is all-consuming but is expressed as a call to the church as the bride of Christ 'to be on fire with a holy love'.[34]

Quite clearly the postmodern paths toward inwardness and mysticism on the one hand, and activism in the world on the other, are at home in Hildegard's scheme. The trick is to amalgamate them in the way of Hildegard: holistic prophetic engagement with God and the world, monastery and church; private contemplation and public role; the tension between the private and the public self maintained, the inward turned outward for the common good. These traits in Hildegard are seen in Bonhoeffer, the man for the moment, who undid the fabric of received wisdom in the German academy and church, reworking the material into something new for such a time as that.

Dietrich Bonhoeffer: Voice of One Man

> Iron sharpens iron,
> and one person sharpens the wits of another (Prov. 27:17).

Like Hildegard, Bonhoeffer was born into a cultured, well-connected, intellectual and influential family. And here ends the similarity between the ways in which the two lives were lived. Unlike the seer's rural upbringing and subsequent withdrawal into the monastery, Bonhoeffer spent his early formative years in the stimulus of the city of Berlin, a melting pot of political, philosophical and religious thought. His undergraduate theological studies were conducted at the University of Tübingen; his graduate studies and lectureship were in the Faculty of Theology in the University of Berlin until the age of 30, when his authorization to

teach was withdrawn by the state. His political activism led to his
involvement with conspirators from within the highest levels of
the German *Abwehr*. He experienced harassment and surveillance
by the state until his house arrest, imprisonment and execution by
the Gestapo at the age of 41.

Iron sharpens iron. Bonhoeffer's life seems to be patterned
according to new sets of spiritual and academic breakthroughs
and punctured by troublesome circumstances of the day. The two
factors sharpen one another and can only fail to trap him in an
ivory tower and to catapult him out instead into church and
world, as a contextual prophetic theologian. The first phase of his
life shows Bonhoeffer as an academic theologian who engages
with the concrete nature of the gospel as student and university
lecturer (1927–33). The second period consists in his vocational
commitment as a theologian, pastor and teacher in a war zone
(1933–40). The third and final stage is his undertaking, as a free
citizen and as a prisoner, to examine Christianity without religion
(1940–45). These three chronological segments of his work do not
correspond precisely with the chapters of this book, as my intention is to explore Bonhoeffer as a prophet, and the study is a the-
matic one. However, there is an imprecise progression, between
the intervals which frame his life and the structure of this book,
which is based on the premise that there is continuity and not dis-
continuity in his writings. Chapter 1 investigates his theological
tipping points as a younger man and poses the questions which
will plague him until their timely airing in the prison correspondence. We then consider the way in which he draws on material
from the pastoral middle period as he applies Scripture to the
traumatic German situation. We follow his passion in the middle
period for costly discipleship, which proceeds in a natural flow
into the final stage of the prison letters – staying with Christ at
the cross – and unpicks a central thread, the open-ended question
of the relation of Christ to real life in a world come of age.
Bonhoeffer is a work in progress. Many have attempted to capture his brilliance and will continue to do so. This book does not
pretend to be anything other than short, sharp jabs at his thinking.

As we track his theological output and the emergent trends he
so vehemently contested, we begin to identify their sophisticated

intricacies which for us, a generation later, are commonplace and no longer innovative: Jesus Christ is no more or less than a fine teaching example to emulate; revelation is not given straight down from a transcendent God but is aided by a mix of the human and divine; God's revelation in Jesus Christ is high up and untouchable somewhere in a refined cultured air; justification by faith is an inner piety without relation to the world as we know it; the door between the secular and spiritual is closed. As we navigate his philosophical course we start to see the drift towards life without God: the door between science and faith no longer ajar but firmly closed; people as inhabitants of a world come of age with no need of God; the church struggling to recover a relevant message for the secular arena and doing it without the Bible.

Academy

Bonhoeffer's theological critique begins within the academy, moves to the edges, works outside it and ends within a prison cell. This time capsule, energized by life experience, sensitizes his awareness and invigorates his consciousness. In our generation, which is accustomed to the interplay and, at times, the integration of world and church, we may feel that Bonhoeffer's stance is too austere. Within the span of a short life he writes and speaks over-abundantly as a contextual prophet of conscience. His view of the conscience is, however, not altogether straightforward. He recognizes that conscience is flawed and beset by sin, by a separation from the other and from God. It is, therefore, not to be trusted. Preoccupation with the search for authentic selfhood and inner conviction is at the expense of the other, and of God. Conscience never realizes a completely pure action and can lead to self-justification and self-delusion. Despite these pitfalls Bonhoeffer advises never to act against the conscience but to surrender all responsible ethical action to the justification of Christ.[35]

Crisis of the word

Bonhoeffer's theological formation is shaped at the outset by external societal forces. At the beginning of his academic career he is, philosophically, a child of the Enlightenment, a product of the age of reason declared by Immanuel Kant (1724–1804) as 'the emergence of man from immaturity that he is himself responsible for. Immaturity is the incapacity to use one's own intelligence without the guidance of another person'.[36] The signature of mature, adult intellectual achievement is autonomous free-wheeling individualism. Theologically Bonhoeffer critiques the inadequacy of the liberal agenda for the sustenance of spiritual life, probably because the intellectual and cultural groups which he describes are his milieu and he identifies with their plight of spiritual alienation. In a paper entitled 'Spiritual Care' he bemoans their fate: 'The cultured are among the most isolated people of our age. They've become distant from the church through a century-long process of individualization and intellectualization. Their spiritual home is liberalism. But in the last decades even this has offered little ground for a spiritual existence. The air became too thin to sustain life and the foundations were not capable enough.'[37]

Bonhoeffer was not only an intellectual adherent of the Christian faith, but also an able practitioner in parish ministry. Nevertheless, he had to undergo a transformative awakening to personal faith in the heart, a revelation *sola fide*, by faith alone. After a religious upbringing and an intensive university career in philosophy and theology, he became a Christian. As the Bible came alive for Bonhoeffer, so likewise did an entire set of convictions which recharged his writing with zeal for the historic times in which he lived. On 27 January 1936, in a letter to a friend, Elisabeth Zinn, he recounts his encounter with the Bible while studying at the Union Theological Seminary, USA:

> I plunged into work in a very unchristian way . . . Then something happened, something that has changed and transformed my life to the present day. For the first time I discovered the Bible . . . I had often preached, I had seen a great deal of the church, spoken and preached about it . . . but I had not yet become a Christian . . . Also I had never prayed, or prayed only very little . . . Then the Bible, and in particular the Sermon on the Mount, freed me from that. Since then everything has changed.[38]

Crisis of revelation

The notion that God's revelation of truth occurs by faith alone is a governing principle in Bonhoeffer's life and thought. This concept produces an obvious synergy between his programmes and the controversial Swiss Reformed theologian Karl Barth (1888–1968), who had erupted into the liberal academy like Vesuvius with the commentary, *The Letter to the Romans*, in 1918. Barth's dialectical or crisis theology confronts the commonly held view at the time that salvation is a question of ethical religious behaviour and not the study of the word of God. Barth's insistence that there can be no 'point of contact' between human nature and God's revelation sets dialectical theology as a plumb line to measure the rightness of religious suppositions. This basis for revelation challenged the 'Luther Renaissance' in 1917 in the Berlin academy, which strove to interpret the new life as a new nature, as 'religious transcendentalism' (Reinhold Seeberg) and a life based on imitation and moralization (Karl Holl).[39] Bonhoeffer wishes to discuss the question of revelation as a *theological* rather than a psychological investigation of consciousness and conscience, contra his teachers.

Bonhoeffer's dissent from the views of his teachers was presented at the University of Berlin in his *Habilitation*, the lecture given for qualification as a university teacher, the argument published as *Act and Being* in 1929. His starting point is that revelation is not an abstraction but an encounter, a free act of God. He rejects the notion of the human potentiality of knowledge of God and the ability of the heart to receive divine revelation of its own accord. His challenge is to Seeberg, an advocate of the 'compelling ability' of humans to receive God into themselves as a 'mould' into which divine revelation is poured. Bonhoeffer states that divine revelation is reliant upon a supernatural action of God, which is the cause of faith: 'If revelation is to come to human beings, they need to be changed entirely. Faith itself must be created in them'.[40]

Bonhoeffer's early discovery and acceptance of Barthian crisis theology did not merely provide a framework for investigating his private spiritual encounter with the Bible, or even a debating tool for his dialogue with theological abstraction in the academy, but an arsenal which equipped him as a spokesperson for justice in his forays into the political life of Nazi Germany. In the contemporary spiritual climate where anything goes and the word of preaching is sometimes no more than an ethical treatise or a light-hearted homily, Bonhoeffer's absorption with the speaking Christ may seem a little over the top. In what follows we relate briefly the primary notion of crisis theology as the Word of God bringing down revelation from above, and Bonhoeffer's application of the living, speaking Word to the situations of his day.

Crisis theology

The primary concern of Barth's crisis theology is the Word of Christ in the burden of preaching. It is a theology by a preacher for preachers. Crisis theology begins with the speaking God who has spoken in Jesus Christ; the 'crisis' is the 'assault of God's Word on the world'. The absoluteness of the Word is non-negotiable: 'That there is a true religion is an event in the act of the grace of God in Jesus Christ. To be more precise, it is an event in the outpouring of the Holy Spirit. To be even more precise, it is an event in the existence of the church and the children of God'.[41]

For Barth, the Word has three meanings: firstly, Jesus Christ is the Word of God applied in a general sense to the whole Bible. The phrase 'the gospel of Jesus Christ' pertains to that which is known through the life, death and resurrection of Christ. Secondly, it is the living, incarnate Word, Jesus Christ, to whom the human words of the Bible testify, but which cannot completely express the fullness of the divine Word. Thirdly, the Word is Jesus Christ, as the being of the church, the Word spoken in revelation, that is, Scripture and preaching.

The new theology settles the Word in its distinctive preaching expression but it also asserts the independent character of the subject of theology. Barth's *Letter to the Romans* is a challenge to the theological programme which accommodates itself to the idea of objective knowledge or a 'science of faith' which denies the biblical revelation of the Faith. Barth argues against that particular agenda. He reasons that the main contents of Christianity are given by revelation and that the paradoxes of faith must be held in dialectical tension. The dialectical approach grasps the paradox of something being both 'yes' and 'no', self-contradictory, or contrary to perceived opinion. It embraces all the 'oddities' of the biblical revelation, the impossible, incredible or marvellous.[42]

The critical point

Bonhoeffer's lecture in 1931, 'The Theology of Crisis and Its Attitude toward Philosophy and Science', is a compelling discussion of the critical point of Barth's dialectic, namely, revelation straight from above in the person of the crucified Christ. If theology has to do with the question of how to speak of God, then in Barthian dialectic 'we stand on an entirely different and new point of departure of the whole problem'.[43]

Bonhoeffer grasps the tricky nettle of transcendent revelation, intractable to the religious thinking of the academy at that time and still hotly contested today, 'But now the Christian message comes: entirely from outside of the world of sin God Himself came in Jesus Christ'. Salvation is an historic event, 'a revelation of God's real acting for mankind in history, a revelation of a new indicative. It is not a new "you ought" but "you are". In other words the revelation of God is executed not in the realm of ideas, but in the realm of history.' Bonhoeffer summarizes the entry of God into history, the incarnation, death and resurrection of Christ, as being contrary to all human potentiality and incompatible with the core of our humanity. In a theme which will become pivotal to his later thought, Bonhoeffer pinpoints the affirmative/negative dialectic in the God who reveals but also hides himself in the 'awkwardness and foolishness' of revelation (cf. Matt. 11:6; 1 Cor. 1). Revelation 'in concealment, secrecy' is disclosed by the faith 'which sees God coming most closely to man where a man hanging on the cross dies in despair with the loud cry: "my God, my God, why hast Thou forsaken me?" Mark 15:34'.

The critical point, with which many of us today in evangelical traditions would agree, is that revelation is not a set of abstract or ethical ideas, but an encounter situated concretely in the person of Jesus Christ. In an introductory paper of 1932/3 on the question of Karl Barth and his theology of the present time Bonhoeffer tackles the problem of philosophical abstraction: 'Theology does not provide rules for life but records revelation in terms of abstractions while the church, on the other hand, must preach, that is to say, proclaim concretely'.[44] The reality of Jesus Christ is, for Bonhoeffer, the whole and complete answer for life: 'Because the world has its being "through Christ" and "for Christ" (Col. 1) every consideration for the human being "per se" or of the world and its order "per se" is an abstraction'.[45] The person of Christ is not an abstract idea but an event, an inbreaking into the real world of the human being. The notion of the invasion of Christ as Word of God is described as an encounter of a concrete nature: 'In as much as Christ commands, he makes very concrete commands'.[46] The call of God comes in the concrete situation: 'The concrete situation in the moment of the divine call'.[47] Bonhoeffer's task is to marry the personal and ethical biblical command to the particular situation in which the one called is found at the moment of the call.

In the period between the two world wars Bonhoeffer's newly found discourse becomes a theological weapon for his battle against the prevailing liberalizing tendencies of the German school. His belief that Scripture is an instrument for the redemptive purposes of God flies in the face of a humanizing programme which uses the Bible as a manual for abstract worldly and ethical principles. His project of concretizing the Bible in the predicaments of the day leads to greater outspokenness on political matters and becomes the tipping point which finally edges him from teaching responsibilities in the academy.

The tipping point

Crisis theology is a springboard for Bonhoeffer's task of realignment, the revelation of the word of God to the human situation in every respect. For Bonhoeffer the moral project is to engage justice, not in a generalized, idealistic way, but in specific issues. It is to read the Bible and to read the world at the same time. The unfettered word is permitted to break in to create a crisis in the reality of the moment. The gravity of purpose in the meshing of word and world is a powerful impetus in Bonhoeffer. The stimulus of crisis theology is in the primacy of God's word for the preaching task; the 'problem of concretion' is his motivating force.[48]

Extracts from two of Bonhoeffer's sermons illustrate the way in which the preaching moment becomes a moment of crisis for the hearer. A sermon on Luke 16:19–31 on the poor of the world confronts religious piety: 'We must put an end to this insolent and hypocritical spiritualising of the gospel. Either take it for what it really is or hate it, but be honest about it'.[49] A sermon at the London Reformed Church on 2 Corinthians 12:9 on the untouchables of society is a manifesto of liberation: 'Christianity stands or falls with its revolutionary protest against violence, arbitrariness and pride of power and with its plea for the weak'.[50]

In the tension of a climate of war, Bonhoeffer views Barth's theology as a new reading of Scripture: 'This is not war psychosis but listening to God's Word'.[51] He is armed with the word of God, a potentially explosive missile in a volatile country: 'Indeed, the word of God is living and active, sharper than any two-edged sword, piercing until it divides soul from spirit, joints from marrow; it is able to judge the thoughts and intentions of the heart' (Heb. 4:12).

Bonhoeffer's diagnosis of situations is prophetically clear-eyed: 'It is only when we look at reality with clear eyes and without any illusion about our morality or our culture that we can believe. Otherwise our faith becomes an illusion'.[52] His moral clear-eyed viewpoint on responsible action means that a prior loyalty to the truth of God's word will bring division within the church, as is made plain in the following letter to Canon Leonard Hodgson, general secretary of the World Conference on Faith and Order, between 1 July 1935 and 26 July 1935:

> Being a member of the Confessional Church I cannot attend an ecumenical conference unless it either excludes the Reich Church or ventures openly to charge both the Reich Church and the Confessional Church with responsibility. This, however, means actually to interfere in their conflict and effectively to pronounce a judgment based upon allegiance to the Word of God and duly established in the name of God's whole communion.[53]

This letter is written in the context of the *Kirchenkampf*, the church struggle between the Confessing Church, founded at the synods of Barmen (31 May 1934) and Dahlem (20 October 1934), and the Reich Church/German Christian Movement, leaning on Nationalist Socialist ideology. Bonhoeffer is unable to dialogue with the Confessional Church unless it throws down the gauntlet to the Reich Church. He appeals to an allegiance to the judging power of Jesus Christ, the Word of God, which supersedes all ecclesiastical or secular projects.

Beyond the academy

In 1936 Bonhoeffer delivered his final series of lectures for the Berlin Faculty of Theology on 'Discipleship', immediately before his authorization to teach at the university was withdrawn. At this juncture he stands, metaphorically speaking, with his back to the gates of the academy and his face outward to the street. These lectures on the Sermon on the Mount demonstrate the effects of the theology of crisis on Bonhoeffer's thinking. The Word comes not as a general truth but as a saying to be obeyed: 'Jesus' concrete call and simple obedience have their own irrevocable meaning. Jesus calls us into a concrete situation in which we can believe in him. That is why he calls in such a concrete way and wants to be so understood, because he knows that people will become free for faith only in concrete obedience'.[54] The book *Discipleship* was published in 1937. The question it poses is the place of Christ in his church in the world. *Discipleship* should be read in the context of the attempt of the Third Reich to conform church, institution and faculties of theology to Nazism and to reserve key positions in the regime for the German Christians, those aligned with Nationalist Socialism.

Bonhoeffer stresses that the church must be a public presence. *Discipleship* articulates the idea of the church as a visible body configured to Christ, taking space (*Raum*) and form (*Gestalt*) in the community.[55] Viewed against the backdrop of Hitler's invasion of Sudetenland on 1 October 1938 and Czechoslovakia on 15 March 1939 in the quest for living space (*Lebensraum*), Bonhoeffer's wording is contentious: 'the church-community claims a physical space here on earth not only for its worship and its order, but also for the daily life of its members. That is why we must now speak of the *living space* (*Lebensraum*) of the visible church-community'.[56] By means of the seminal text, Acts 2:47, 'And day by day the Lord added to their number those who were being saved', Bonhoeffer advocates the extension of church boundaries in the aggressive language of invasion: 'This visible church-community whose reality fully extends to all areas of life invades the world and snatches its children. The daily growth of the church-community demonstrates the power of the Lord who dwells in its midst'.[57] This statement refuses to accept any Nazi attempts to control church politics.

The theological standpoint of the Confessing Church signalled for Bonhoeffer the true visible church whose membership was marked out by its beliefs. According to this stance, therefore, a non-member of the Confessing Church could be excluded from salvation. Bonhoeffer works out his premise on the old maxim that 'outside of the church there is no salvation' (*extra ecclesiam nulla salus*): 'The question of church membership is the question of salvation. The boundaries of the church are the boundaries of salvation. Whoever knowingly cuts himself off from the Confessing Church in Germany cuts himself off from salvation'.[58] Bonhoeffer emphasizes that the unity between Christ and his church is a bond of salvation, not a mystical fusion or an institution.

The implication of the union between Christ and church is stated in Bonhoeffer's paper, 'On the Question of the Church Community', written on 21 April 1936.[59] The Bible study in the paper, 'The Reconstruction of Jerusalem according to Ezra and Nehemiah', deals with the problem of the authority of existing church communities if they are at variance with the theological position of the Confessing Church. Bonhoeffer maintains the unity of the church, but clearly states that the true church is known in the way it receives God's pledges: 'The church is one now and then . . . But where the promise of God is perceived and earnestly seized, there will be the church'.[60]

From our short interaction with Bonhoeffer we become aware that he wrote within a crucible of war and that his works are situated within a context which, in the main, is not our experience in the western church. We may feel concern that his strong views on the church raise issues of exclusivity and the problem of breakaway congregations who claim to be the true church. This radical attitude is certainly not that of Hildegard, for whom the Catholic Church was a bulwark within which the Benedictine Rule was lived and outworked, despite its apparent weaknesses. It is, however, important to remember that at every turn Bonhoeffer acted in response to his context, not in a knee-jerk reaction, but after careful and considered theological reflection.

Rebel community

The breakaway Finkenwalde seminary, an experimental project of the Confessing Church, was in itself a prophetic sign of contradiction, a political conspiracy. *Life Together* was published in 1938 as a retrospective commentary on the seminary, which was established in 1935 and closed by the police in 1937 with the arrest of twenty-seven seminarians. The genesis of *Life Together*, therefore, is not church or academy but a subversive seminary in the spiritual heartland of the crucible of a nation on the brink of war. For the rebel *koinonia* intent on making a collective impact on the political wasteland, Scripture was a reliable resource. *Life Together* demonstrates the dialectic of the word in tension with the political pressures of Nazi Germany. It is a devotional training manual for young men living in community under the Bible as their guiding principle.

In a letter to Barth, Bonhoeffer expresses himself as a far-sighted visionary for theological training: 'But there are very few who recognize this sort of work with young theologians as a task of the church and do something about it'.[61] The founding of the Finkenwalde seminary arose from his conviction that the future of the church's work lay in 'the entire formation of the new generation of theologians' through 'church and cloister schools in which pure doctrine, the Sermon on the Mount and the cultus are taken seriously'.[62] The statement of purpose of the Finkenwalde seminary co-ordinates theological reflection with prayer and acts of service: 'Here they are to think through the basic questions of Holy Scripture, practical work and true evangelical teaching with the cooperation of the director of the seminary. The young brethren will thus engage in a common Christian life of daily devotions together, quiet times for prayer, and mutual service'.[63] In a memorandum advocating foreign student exchange, he notes that the mutual benefit of such an interchange 'lies in the close common life of a brotherhood of theologians'.[64]

Bonhoeffer's interest in communities ranged from black Harlem churches to a Benedictine monastery. The establishment of the Finkenwalde seminary signifies an attempt at a revolutionary act of recovery of the monastic tradition. The particular element taken from monastic tradition is the shape of the day:

> Life together under the Word begins at an early hour of the day with a worship service together. A community living together gathers for praise and thanks, Scripture reading, and prayer. The

profound silence of morning is first broken by the prayer and song of the community of faith. After the silence of the night and early morning, hymns and the Word of God will be heard all the more clearly. Along these lines the Holy Scriptures tell us that the first thought and the first word of the day belong to God: 'O Lord, in the morning you hear my voice; in the morning I plead my case to you, and watch' (Ps. 5:4).[65]

It is an interesting point of similarity between Hildegard and Bonhoeffer to note the 'harmonious echoes' between Benedictine monastic practice and the experimental Finkenwalde community life.[66] *The Rule of St Benedict* sets out a frame of participation in the life of Christ: 'Never swerving from its instructions, then, but faithfully observing his teaching in the monastery until death, we shall through patience share in the sufferings of Christ that we may deserve also to share in his kingdom'.[67] *Life Together* engages with this theme of participation: 'Our community consists solely in what Christ has done to both of us . . . I have community with others and continue to have it only through Jesus Christ . . . we have one another only through Christ, but through Christ we really do *have* one another. We have one another completely and for all eternity'.[68] The primary stance in the *Rule* is listening: 'Listen carefully, my son, to the master's instructions, and attend to them with the ear of your heart'.[69] *Life Together* stipulates that 'Just as there are certain times in a Christian's day for speaking the Word, particularly the time of daily worship and prayer together, so the day also needs certain times of silence under the Word and silence that comes out of the Word. These will mainly be the times before and after hearing the Word'.[70]

Concepts seminal to the monastic discipline which are found in *The Imitation of Christ* by Thomas à Kempis (1379–1471) are mirrored in *Life Together*.[71] *The Imitation of Christ* states: 'In silence and quiet the devout soul advances in virtue and learns the hidden truths of scripture'.[72] The text, 'No one is safe in speaking unless he loves to be silent', finds an echo in *Life Together*: 'No one speaks more confidently than the one who gladly remains silent'.[73] Allusions in *Life Together* to *The Imitation of Christ* are to be found in the sentiment that God is sought not for personal advantage or self-seeking, but for God alone: 'Seek God, not happiness'.[74] *The*

Imitation of Christ urges: 'The true lover of Christ, however, who sincerely pursues virtue, does not fall back upon consolations nor seek such pleasure of sense, but prefers severe trials and hard labours for the sake of Christ'.[75] In practising the ministry of meekness to all the brothers in Christ *Life Together* exhorts: 'I must not raise myself above them'.[76] *The Imitation of Christ* reflects, 'Hence, you must not think that you have made any progress until you look upon yourself as inferior to all others'.[77]

Radical edge

The works *Discipleship, Life Together* and *Prayer Book of the Bible* (1940) are written in a pastoral genre by a practitioner of spirituality rooted in the guild of biblical theologians. Bonhoeffer is not only a hearer of the word but a doer of it, and he teaches others to do the same (Jas 1:22). All, however, is not plain sailing in the sea of faith. Whereas the theology of crisis is adequate for Bonhoeffer's task of revelation as encounter, it is inadequate for his project of binding Christ firmly to the communities of both church and world. Despite his admiration for Barth and the impact of the new theology on his study of the Bible, Bonhoeffer's critique of Barth is his failure to link God with sufficient seriousness to the world. He complains that for Barth God is always 'coming' and never simply 'there', that he removes God in his transcendent majesty right out of the human domain: 'God is always the God who "comes" and never the God who "is there"'.[78]

Bonhoeffer's work *Ethics*, published in 1940, begins to tease out what it means to drive God closer to the world. Bonhoeffer agrees with Barth that God in Christ stands over and against the world because he is the Lord of the world. For Bonhoeffer, however, the boundaries of the church must incorporate the world. If Christ is total reality, then he must be Lord over the two realities of sacred and secular, and these two fields of truth become one entity.[79] Bonhoeffer's unremitting theological task is to concretize Christ in the church: 'The community is the present Christ himself'.[80] This is a move away from the notion of the free majesty of God, God-being-for-himself, to God-being-in-relation with the world, committed to this world and not aloof from it. God is brought nearer to the world in Jesus Christ: 'In Jesus Christ the word of God and the community-of-God are inextricably bound together'. *Ethics* describes the move toward the worldly Christ. The church is to proclaim God's revelation in Jesus Christ as the one 'in whom God has bodily taken on humanity. Jesus Christ is one in whom there is the new humanity, the Community-of-God'.[81] On these grounds, therefore, Bonhoeffer stresses legitimate openness and responsibility towards the world. These thoughts may not appear particularly extreme to our twenty-first century church concerned to make God present in the community it inhabits, but they are only the first sounds in a score played out to its finale in Bonhoeffer's own life, committed with absoluteness to sharing in the misery of a world without God and leading to his imprisonment and execution.

One Life

The visionary lives of Hildegard and Bonhoeffer are the birth pangs of a new age. Each stands on the cusp of a different horizon. From the midst of an era whose desire for God is trumpeted aloud, Hildegard peers into modernity and the reign of reason. From the centre of an enlightened world gone crazy, Bonhoeffer gathers the scattered bread of revelation, shakes his head at its perversion, and stares ahead at the coming randomness of postmodernism. As a Christian, Bonhoeffer's freedom consists in his capacity to choose an unpopular course, albeit enigmatic, and to resist the pressure of compromise, the coercion of the strong, or the intimidation of the worldly. His is a brave and courageous life which shows us the power of one among the masses. His compelling optimism is not in his characteristic self-confidence or reliance on intellectual mastery or upbringing, neither is he hopeful of always understanding the God he serves. His hope is in a higher promise, 'that now we see in a glass darkly but then face to face'. The heartbeat of Hildegard's prophetic call is the message from God for the people of her day. If Deborah, the Judge, took her seat of prophecy between Ramah, the high place, and Bethel, the house of God (Judg. 4:5), then likewise Hildegard: 'Thus we can say that prophecy dwelt in blessed Hildegard *between the house of God and the high place*, for though it was seen manifest in a particular place, yet it was to be received in a spiritual manner'.[82]

We see that the medieval tradition has great respect for the gift of the Spirit, which is given for the purpose of a higher power of wisdom, and granted in order to enable right judgements. We may compare Hildegard's incredible gift of sight with that of Solomon the wise, the ruler of Israel, who asked for wisdom so that he could discern the ways of the Lord and know the paths he should take. Hildegard's otherworldly enlightenment empowers her to probe the mysteries of divinity with a prophetic charism like that of Joseph, in whom is found the 'spirit of God', the wisdom to fathom the thoughts of God (Gen. 41:38). In the case of Bonhoeffer we find a theologian, a product of the Enlightenment and the age of reason, struggling to make sense of his age and with all the expertise at his disposal determined to sustain the centrality of divine revelation given solely in Jesus Christ. Each life and work embodies a compelling slant on prophecy. Together they are a formidable force.

If the church today embraces *both* the prophetic charism given freely by the Spirit (peculiarities notwithstanding) *and* a rock-like faith in the particularity of God's exposure of himself in Jesus Christ (a somewhat unpopular tenet), there is a real possibility of a broadening of prophetic perspective in both personal and public domains. For practitioners this will mean welcoming prophets in churches. Naturally the undertaking is risk-filled; it entails extra work in setting up accountability structures to ensure that the prophet maintains a life which exhibits the 'testimony of Jesus'. It will mean helping the prophet to gain greater intimacy with Jesus in a disciplined life of prayer and Bible study, alone and with others, so that the gift of prophecy is honed and polished by the Spirit. Above all, the church will learn to love and cherish such visionaries, not to estrange them, as they are gifts to the body of Christ and to the world. We may be harbouring a potential young leader like Joan of Arc, or a political statesman like Nelson Mandela, or a youthful and enterprising Mark Zuckerberg (the founder whiz kid of Facebook), on the cusp of a life of influence for good or ill and in need of nurture and discipleship into maturity.

2.

SCRIPTURE AND VISION

Blessed Lord, who caused all holy Scriptures to be written for our learning: Grant us so to hear them, read, mark, learn, and inwardly digest them, that we may embrace and ever hold fast the blessed hope of everlasting life (Anglican Collect).[1]

The issue which presents itself today for those of us who are preachers and teachers is not one of either prophecy or Scripture, but rather their deeply knit cohesion. Our task is not to study prophecy and the Bible as separate disciplines, but to unleash the prophetical meaning which is embedded in the biblical text itself. Such a prophetical project will be led by the following principle: the dependency on the full operation of the Spirit, not only as the 'finger' of God *then* in the inspiration of the written word, but as a working presence *now*, so that the person of the Word, Jesus Christ, is fully revealed and brought to life for the reader throughout the whole counsel of God. Thus the union of Word and Spirit in the text elicits a prophetical sense for each situation and context. A method of hermeneutics (interpretation of the written text) must be sought, therefore, to assist and not hinder our primary objective of acquiring the spiritual sense in biblical passages, so that preaching and teaching come alive and speak with dynamism into the human condition. It was this search which led Bonhoeffer to throw out the dry historical-critical method of biblical exegesis which dominated the German university academy and to take up a creative pre-modern approach, the practice familiar to Hildegard.

Limitations of the Historical-Critical Method

The historical-critical method, developed from the nineteenth century, rotates round an axis of investigating the wider historical context in the biblical text, finding a primary meaning there and applying it to the present time. There is no special 'spiritual' method for deciphering texts. There are many objections to the usefulness of the historical-critical method among modern biblical scholars. In the field of Old Testament studies, Childs states that it is theologically inadequate for the task of interpretation of the prophets not as foretellers, telling of distant future issues, but as 'forthtellers' who address a concrete historical community of Israelites with political, social and religious issues. Von Balthasar maintains that it has destroyed the old form of the *argumentum ex prophetia*, an exegetical procedure that understood the sayings of the old covenant as a direct prophetic reference to Christ (for example, Isaiah 7:14). Herbert alleges that in the modern alienation from the Old Testament there is a loss of mystical interpretation. Brueggemann argues that it resists normative statements of faith.[2] In general terms Louth protests that it limits and enslaves inspiration, in that exegesis is not simply an objective comment with only one right interpretation but creative engagement between reader and text. Ricoeur asserts that it produced the modern problem of deciphering the New Testament not as an absolute to interpret the Old Testament, but with its own literal meaning. The Bible is desacralized into the word of human beings. As an exegetical method, historical-criticism is a limited tool in the search for the inner meaning of texts. A critical revision of its particular line of development lies in a recovery of patristic-medieval exegesis, which Childs suggests is an attempt to retain the 'coercion or pressure of the biblical text itself'.[3]

If we are to address the problem of congregational boredom with dullness, shallowness, or mind-numbing biblical exposition, which has arisen from too close an adherence to the historical-critical method (or no method at all), preachers and teachers do well to delve into the treasure trove of patristic-medieval exegesis. If we are to recover inspiration for prophetic preaching and teaching, by a discovery of the inner meaning already set into the text by the Holy Spirit, we are required to find again the Christ-focus throughout Scripture and the interlinear relationship between the two testaments. To this we turn as we draw upon the work of Henri de Lubac (1896–1991) who underpins the reflections on Hildegard and Bonhoeffer.

Retrieval of Patristic-Medieval Exegesis

De Lubac was a prominent member of the French *ressourcement* revival who fought against the rising tide of secularism, the lack of a religious or spiritual basis in attitudes and activities in society. Many of his copious research notes were written on the run and kept in a sack during the German occupation of France in the 1940s and during the six months he spent in hiding in 1943. There are resonances with Bonhoeffer in de Lubac's leadership, namely the denunciation of the anti-Christian character of Nazi neo-paganism and anti-Semitism. The quest of both theologians is for a deeper spirituality in the midst of a world war of catastrophic proportions.

In his four-volume work *Medieval Exegesis* (1959–64), de Lubac deals with the modern divide between exegesis and spirituality. He strives to recover the spiritual heritage of the past by an extensive overview of patristic exegesis. Christ is the endpoint of Scripture and brings about the unity of the two testaments. It is the universal belief of the primitive church that Scripture is required to be 'opened' by Christ (Luke 24:45; Rev. 5), or that all Scripture is interpreted through Christ. De Lubac suggests that ancient writers were prophets who 'polished' old truths, and saw the revelation of the Word of God before his coming. Their 'moment' of recognition of the Word of God constitutes the New Testament, and the 'moment' of the New Testament is the 'critical instant', the 'eternal instant', the *kairos* event.[4]

De Lubac shows how multiple meanings are layered in the text when the patristic-medieval pattern of interpretation is used, known as the fourfold sense of Scripture. This is a technique used to analyze the passage firstly as history (literal meaning), secondly as allegory (a means to understand difficult passages), thirdly as tropology (moral sense), fourthly as anagogy (spiritual sense). There is thus a gradual but deliberate ascent to a higher level (anagogy): that is, to the prophetic perspective which looks closely into the temporal historical event and gives to it the spiritual sense already inlaid in the text by the mind of God. God's insertion of himself into textual activity consecrates history and gives it sacred meaning. The church fathers held that God is revealed through history and Scripture is bound to history. Historical realities are understood in a spiritual manner and, conversely, spiritual realities are understood historically. This exegetical system is represented by the two schools of Alexandria and Antioch. Both hold that 'there is a spiritual force in history'; on the one hand, the 'very facts have an inner significance', and in time 'are pregnant with an eternal value' (Alexandria); on the other hand, the reality in Old and New Testaments 'is not merely spiritual, but historical as well' (Antioch).[5] The history of the Old Testament is seen by the church fathers in a spiritual way, as one comprehensive and extensive prophecy, whose subject is Christ. The trials of Job, for example, are at the same time Jesus crucified and his persecuted church.[6]

Hildegard of Bingen: Recovering the Prophetical Way in Scripture

> My heart overflows with a goodly theme;
>> I address my verses to the king;
>> my tongue is like the pen of a ready scribe (Ps. 45:1).

Hildegard's style is crowded with what may seem to us in the twenty-first century to be outdated, old-fashioned and archaic language – similes, metaphors, allusions and the like. These concepts will appear very odd to readership schooled in the literal meaning of the Bible, or those content with a simple 'thought for the day'. Hildegard offers us bouquets of sweet-smelling flowers; a few are plain but many are exotic. We are asked to sniff expectantly and to find in each arrangement a meaning, a certain spiritual 'sense'. In her writings there is much evidence of the fourfold sense of Scripture, especially the meanings of allegory and anagogy. Allegory describes the first 'advent', the coming of Christ as the Word of God into history in the story of salvation.

Anagogy declares the second 'advent', the coming of Christ in his glory in the future to take his own to himself. The minds of the medieval theologians are filled with these two 'advents', these two 'comings' of Christ, both now and then. The expression 'prophetical way' is used by Guibert of Nogent (1053–1124) in conjunction with the oft-repeated phrase, 'in that day'. The term stresses the immediacy of prophetic utterance in the presence of the divine light *now* ('in that day'), but also the certainty and closeness of the second coming of Christ *then* ('in that day').[7] Rupert of Deutz (1079–1129) in his comment on the list of *charismata* (gifts) in 1 Corinthians 14 tells us to nurture the gift of prophecy so that it can assist our Bible study: 'Among the spiritual gifts with which the Holy Spirit enriches his church, we should lovingly cultivate the one which consists in the power to understand what we say in prayer and in psalmody: this is no less than a manner of prophesying.'[8] Hildegard's task is not to alter the text of Scripture but to refresh it, to rewire it in order to impact the recipient with its truth in a new, compelling way. She wants to wake up the church. She writes that her desire is 'to arouse sluggish souls to vigilance' in the manner of David in his 'songs of prophecy and rejoicing'.[9] She is aware that prophecy brings inward self-illumination as a mirror from heaven: 'There will be prophecy; wisdom will be gentle and strong, and all believers will see themselves in it as in a mirror.'[10]

Hildegard's prophetic songs, letters, dreams, drama, verses and scholastic comments are a torrent of images, an overflow of spiritual liveliness, which we may find difficult to decipher although her imagery is not always new. Her sources are hard to find in the tradition or in other writings, because she writes as an unlettered seer and, apart from Scripture, never cites any learned texts explicitly. The source of Hildegard's writing is a vortex of light arising from meditation on Scripture and vision, at the heart of which is a kaleidoscope of allegorical imagery to which we must now attend if we are to understand her prophetic vision.

Allegory

To allegorize is to speak otherwise, to state a meaning in the text which is secret or hidden and not the obvious or literal one. Allegory is a road map to guide and explore the inner worlds of experience and introspection and can be used to navigate spiritual truth. We are not ordinarily moved in a deep way by dry theological doctrine. The cognitive faculties may be active but the whole person may remain unmoved, resisting further engagement. Allegory can impress us and move us into experience by getting to the heart of reality in a way in which theology cannot. It is almost as though most of life is seen from below in 2-D, but when we are acclimatized to an extra dimension we begin to see from above, in 3-D. We can come at truth from above or below. Allegory has an impact which literalism does not. The origins of allegory may be traced to a moral revolution in the latter days of paganism. Contending forces in the inner subjective world are depicted in literature by the only means possible, that of allegory. It begins with something insubstantial, for example, a human passion, and then invents something visible to express the emotion. Thus allegory is a vehicle to represent the immaterial in picturable ways.[11]

Hildegard's visions are a bridge between heaven and earth, a highway from a real and visible known world to another realm altogether. They serve to quicken in us something strange and unfamiliar, to heighten the less real and invisible. She employs allegorical language to expand in writing what she sees in paranormal vision. The images express the inexpressible in a less real way because they speak in a different manner than one would otherwise speak. We shall see, for example, Hildegard's use of the figure of the eagle for the profundity of heavenly vision and the virtues of knowledge, rationality and boldness; the wheel for the Father's eternity; the tunic for the Son's equality with the Father; the Warrior, Champion and light-filled man for the stories of the Redeemer; fire for the bond and concord of the Holy Spirit. The allegorical image, therefore, may be understood as a divine teaching or didactic gift to the prophet to make visible what is seen and heard. The vision is then explained and handed down as a lesson to the church.

Letter 103r[12]
An extract from a letter to Guibert of Gembloux is an example of Hildegard's gambit to unite Scripture with a wealth of empirical observation and speculative imagination. Her spirit soars to interpret what she sees not only in the supernatural, but also in the

natural. She appeals to the monk to use his powers of ingenuity and to look at the flight path of an eagle in a literal, physical way: 'Observe the eagle flying toward the clouds on two wings'. She then points to the fact that if one wing is injured the eagle is grounded: 'If one of those wings is wounded, the eagle falls to earth and cannot rise, no matter how hard it tries'. She then expounds on the human plight, the problem of knowing too much about sin, and uses a picture well-known to her, the two wings of rationality representing the knowledge of good and evil: 'So too man flies with the two wings of rationality, that is to say, with the knowledge of good and evil. The right wing is good knowledge, and the left, evil'. The wings are an allegorical way of speaking otherwise about the tree of the knowledge of good and evil in Eden. The 'two wings of rationality' are God-given, and the neglect of the use of either will lead to a disastrous fall from which, humanly speaking, it will be impossible to recover. This figurative use of the eagle seems to leave the written page with immediacy and to take flight in a prophetic word of encouragement spoken directly into Guibert's life situation: 'Now, dear son of God, may the Lord raise the wings of your knowledge to straight paths so that although you come into contact with sin through the senses . . . you nonetheless never willingly consent to sin'.

Revelation 12:14

The exegesis of Revelation 12:14 shows the first 'coming' of Christ in redemptive history in a pictorial image of raised eagle wings, pointed backwards and forwards. These represent the two testaments, with Christ as the meaning of both and the fulcrum of its historical and spiritual realities: 'But the woman was given the two wings of the great eagle, so that she could fly from the serpent into the wilderness, to her place where she is nourished for a time, and times, and half a time.'

In the tradition with which Hildegard was undoubtedly familiar, Scripture is allegorized as an eagle, the raised wings being the two testaments. In her vision she sees a winged man with four wings. The additional pair on back and front gives greater power to interpret the two testaments. This is a lesson for those who teach, as it highlights the gift of superior divine knowledge granted through prophecy:

> And behold on each shoulder he had one wing which covered his arms and also one wing on his back and one wing on his chest which were all raised as if for flying. The wing which was on his back, at its extreme point, was just bending to the left wing and not to the right wing. But the wing which was at his chest, at its extreme point, was more-or-less divided into two parts in such a way that one part was curving backwards towards the left wing and the other part towards the right wing. And in the middle of each wing one book became visible.[13]

Hildegard's interpretation of the vision raises several interesting points. The raised wings ready to fly indicate that revelation has already begun and teachers can take courage that they shall be inspired in their difficult task, which is to draw up never-ending truth as if from a well which never runs dry. The wings on back and chest are hidden mysteries, which 'teachers of truth now try to uncover . . . as if from a well . . . they will never be strong enough to empty this well'. The revelation, however, is incomplete. A mere glimpse of what is to come is hinted at by the tip of the wing on the back which points to the left wing, that is, the Law and the Prophets in the Old Testament, but does not yet touch the right wing, the light of truth in the New Testament, 'because that side does not yet worship the one who sends forth heavenly rewards'. The wing on the chest with parts curving in different directions points to the left wing, to the former works in the Old Testament which defended earthly things (circumcision) and can now be abandoned for the right wing, the eagerly awaited heavenly things (baptism of the Spirit). The message of the vision is: the old has gone, the new has come; cast off the law and take on Christ. There is an echo of the same idea in lines from Hildegard's 'Hymn to Saint Ursula':

> For the Law showed Moses
> God's back but veiled his face.[14]

Anagogy

The use of anagogy is probably a little less familiar to us than that of the more easily discernible allegory. In this method we engage with underlying meanings in the text before us. In the study of anagogy a church father of importance is Origen (184/5–253/4). He uses anagogy as a ladder to climb up to the higher, spiritual, prophetic, figurative sense, to ascend from the letter to the spirit, from the figures or images to the truth. For Origen and other patristic and medieval writers it is prophecy which reveals the ultimate meaning of history and all temporal events. Everything coheres in God, who has already inserted into historic happenings their significance, which prophecy unfolds as a scroll is unfurled. The Bible communicates not only with the narrative of words but also with events. Things – the people and events – have a figurative dimension beyond words which transcends time and enthuses prophetic or apocalyptic insight for ages to come, which is the anagogical sense. We find in Hildegard a dense proliferation of anagogical imagery which follows Origen's prophetical way. An example is in the following piece of writing, which causes us to peer behind the metaphor of a musical 'Sound', to the idea of Christ, the very first 'Voice', and to draw from the image a universal meaning for all time. In this prophetic meditation on the 'comings' of Christ, Hildegard climbs a metaphorical ladder from his 'coming' into the spiritual chaos in Germany at the time (the temporal thing or event), up to the ultimate meaning of his 'coming' into history at the end of the age. It shows how meditation on Scripture – in this case, John 1:3,14 and Genesis 1:10,26 – informs the seer's ongoing prophetic prospect.

Meditation 374[15]
The short Meditation on Christ, the Word of God, found in the collection of *Letters* is structured around themes of the centrality of the Word in God's creative act, the significance of the Word in the temporal event of redemption, the prophetic word announced as revelation for the day – past, present and future – and a concluding plea for mercy to the Author of all time. Hildegard's meditation on a clutch of biblical verses extracts a higher prophetic reality lying dormant in the texts and transposes them into a new key, so that the new Sound, 'in that day', is not only for today but also for the day before and the days to come. The first extract allegorizes the Word as First Sound of God:

The First Sound that came forth from God remained until it restored the human race in a virgin's womb. This is the Word, as John witnesses, through which 'all things were made' [John 1:3] according to their kind. Then, God made man to his 'image and likeness' [Gen. 1:26], and he also created the birds, the animals, and the fish to serve mankind. For the angels and the spirits of the blessed are in God's presence. But because the Word came forth from God, God the Father named it 'Son', for the Word was begotten by God, and it was life.

The timeless Word is a vibration in eternity, an utterance at the beginning of the creation in the first time-zone and sounding until the Sound is birthed in the Virgin and humanity renewed. This feather-light image, like an electric impulse, resonates again in one of Hildegard's prayers, in praise to the Creator:

O earliest Voice
Through which all creatures were created[16]

Hildegard's musings on the threefold operation of the Trinity in the work *Scivias* produces a similar musical note:

A word is composed of sound, force and breath. A word has sound in order to be heard, force in order to be understood, breath in order to be completed. In the sound of the word consider the Father, who expresses all things by his ineffable power; in the force of the word consider the Son, marvellously engendered of the Father; in the breath of the word consider the Holy Spirit, who burns gently within them.[17]

In *Divine Works* the Sound of God enters earthly creatures to enliven them too: 'For when the Word of God sounded, this Word appeared in every creature, and this sound was life in every creature'.[18] Meditation 374 continues with a reflection on time past when the Word became flesh, his tent pitched, habitable in the world because God desires union with the creatures he had made in his image (John 1:14): 'And the Word, through which "all things were made", was incarnated in the world, for God wished to be joined to mankind, because he had made man in his own image. Therefore, I who live say: In the first age, I created that which was pleasing to me [cf. Gen. 1:10]'. The 'first age' signifies the creation which is very pleasing to God (Gen. 1:10). However, it is also the historic age before Christ, as Hildegard declares in Letter 15r: the 'first age' was pleasing as the age of prefiguring, of 'luminaries' with good doctrine and exemplary lives, the priest Abel, the papal offices of Noah, the prophet Moses.[19] There is nothing unfamiliar about this basic doctrine, but then in a flash Hildegard introduces an obscure and random prophetic thought into the Meditation and we stumble into anagogy: 'Afterward, when the world reached the midpoint, it came nigh on to ruin. What will follow is hidden.'

When exactly is the midpoint when the world faced melt-down and between which markers in history did it occur? Is the answer to Hildegard's question concealed also from the prophet? Letter 77r has a similar theme: 'But the time of great strain and destruction has not yet arrived . . . Nevertheless, the present age is still a time most vile. Therefore, look to times past, consider how honourable they were . . . Indeed, a time of right-eousness and morality will come soon, a time which will look back to the first dawn.'[20] This is most likely to be a reference to a coming catastrophe involving Henry IV (1054–1106), whom Hildegard branded a worshipper of Baal and held responsible for the weakened state of the church. In a sermon preached to the clergy at Trier between 1160 and 1161 she thunders: 'Now, however, manly fortitude has degenerated into womanish weak-ness . . . This womanish time began under a certain tyrant, from whom every evil came forth'.[21] In a letter to the prelates at Mainz between 1178 and 1179 Hildegard has no hesitation in declaring herself God's warrior: 'This time is a womanish time, because the dispensation of God's justice is weak. But the strength of God's justice is exerting itself, a female warrior battling against injustice, so that it might fall defeated'.[22] Nevertheless, however deeply Hildegard may feel about her role as God's fighter for justice, God's prophet, she is committed firstly to the truth of the written word and in submission to it knows that a human being, however righteous, however devoted to justice, cannot save: 'Even if these three men – Noah, Daniel and Job – were in it, they could save only themselves by their righteousness [Ezek. 14:14]'.

The closing invocation appeals to a divine warrior to arise and deliver (Germany or the Holy Roman Empire?) from the catastrophe to come: 'Woe, woe, O "man of war" [Is. 42:13], rise up and, in your just judgments, seek out whatever may keep ruin from coming. You will remain "king for ever" [Ps. 29:10], but we are feeble and weak. Have mercy on us.' Hildegard prays prophetically from Scripture, pleading for the divine combatant, the 'mighty warrior' who can forestall the coming disaster: 'The Lord will march out like a mighty man, like a warrior, he will stir up his zeal. With a shout he will raise the battle cry and will triumph over his enemies' (Isa. 42:13).

Jesus Christ is the mighty warrior who defeats his ancient enemy, Satan, the 'old combatant'.[23] The closing line, 'You will hold out, King forever', reverberates with the opening line of the Meditation. The prophet has complete confidence that the Sound of Christ which began the world will also preserve the world to its end. It is little wonder that Hildegard's writings have been ransacked by researchers eager for predictions about the end of the world. More to the point, however, is her admonition of powerful political figures on the world stage as it was then, not as prophetic utterance pulled from the air, but as an acute response to the written scriptural text.

Meditation on Scripture

For us today, heavily laden with information and accustomed to a multitude of aids to assist our reading of Scripture, Hildegard's method may strike us as oversimplified or unsophisticated, perhaps even intellectually barren. She read Scripture as one enclosed within the constraints and limits of her time. She was enfolded, firstly, as a believer in the inspiration of the whole of Scripture. She was cloistered, secondly, as a Benedictine nun, subject to the monastic discipline of psalmody, the divine offices, and meditation. These two 'confinements' might appear suffocating to the popular postmodern quest for the freedom of the arbitrary, the erratic, the eclectic, the diverse, the unfenced-in limitless horizon of speech and text. On the contrary, however, the captivity by the text itself *within the* regular recitation, reading and receiving of Scripture is a liberating force. Psalm 1:2–3 sings the praises of one who loves to ruminate on the law of God. This love of learning and the desire for God is at the heart of the monastic age of which Hildegard was a part. The psalmist sums up the fruit of the labour of contemplation as reaping a considerable reward:

> Their delight is in the law of the LORD,
>   and on his law they meditate day and night.
> They are like trees
>   planted by streams of water,
> which yield their fruit in its season,
>   and their leaves do not wither.
> In all that they do, they prosper.

Hildegard's Bible study was governed by two medieval principles: the first an unquestioned premise about the authority of Scripture, the second a daily practice of *lectio divina* (divine reading). Firstly, the uncomplicated patristic-medieval view of the divine origins of the Bible as simply the work of the Holy Spirit is enunciated by the early church father Augustine (396–430). Scripture is the second book of creation: 'Moreover, the Holy Spirit, the "finger of God", who had already shaped the letters of creation, went back to work in order to draft this new book. He unfurled the heavens of Scripture. He spread out this second firmament, which, like the first, recounts God's power and also his mercy, the latter of which it is much better at showing than is the first book.'[24] The inspiration of Scripture is guaranteed by its Author, who lives in it and whose breath has always animated it. This principle of divine authority is enunciated by Gregory the Great (590–604): 'Who wrote the work it is completely superfluous to ask since by faith its author is believed to have been the Holy Spirit. The One who dictated that it be written wrote it himself.'[25]

For the devoted monastic it followed that, if the 'finger of God' wrote the Bible, its message is ever ready to be rewritten by the Spirit in the mind and heart of the one reading. The passage for meditation comes alive and is quickened internally so that each word, phrase or sentence carries a communication from God for the well-being of the soul.

Secondly, the impact of the unremitting exercise of *lectio divina*, the act of reading and meditating slowly and deeply upon the words of Scripture, is a muscular, physical act of engagement of musing under the breath or out loud. Here there is a close attachment to the text itself; without the use of notes or commentaries the eyes scrutinize the passage, the spirit and heart strive for its meaning, and the ears are inwardly attuned to the voice of God in the sacred page. This monastic love of learning is not for the sake of knowledge which puffs up, but for the beauty of relationship with God. The desire for God is the way of contrition, of love, of personal experience, of admiration. Thus John Cassian (360–d.c.430s) describes the repetition of the words of the psalms not only as past prophecy but as present prophetic fulfilment in the heart of the reader:

> He will begin to repeat them and to treat them in his profound compunction of heart not as if they were composed by the prophet but as if they were his own utterances and his own prayer. Certainly he will consider that they are directed to his own person, and he will recognize that their words were not only achieved by and in the prophet in times past but that they are daily borne out and fulfilled in him.[26]

With the practice of the *lectio divina* Hildegard enjoyed a daily baptism in the word of God, a total immersion in the stream of Scripture, so that living water drawn from its depths irrigated her own dry soul and yielded a crop of goodness for others. Here the sanctification by Christ of the soul is achieved through the word in Scripture. He gave himself for the church 'in order to make her holy by cleansing her with the washing of water by the word' (Eph. 5:26).

Monastic liturgical discipline enshrines Scripture not only as *read* but also as *heard* in sermons and teaching and as timeless truths repeatedly chanted and sung in the psalms, canticles, verses and stories of the liturgical offices.

Luke 19:41–47[27]

In the move to the Rupertsberg convent in 1150 Hildegard expanded her practice of written biblical commentary and established a venue for the practice of oral exegesis. This was probably the site for the production of the collection of *Gospel Homilies*, her sermons and teachings delivered to her nuns in a regular pattern. These constitute a running commentary on each phrase of the gospel text for the day. Two of these sermons and teachings concerned Catharism. Hildegard's nuns preserved the texts of her talks and sermons to them. She was a preacher not only in the convents she established but also in her public mission trips. Her written homilies illustrate the way in which a spiritual interpretation of Scripture may be extracted from a text whose interpretation is well known and familiar. Such a passage is Hildegard's Trinitarian emphasis in the homily on Luke 19:41–47, the story of the expulsion by Jesus of the temple money-changers. The first division in the homily shows the moment of creation to the time of Christ's teaching. Here Jesus' weeping represents the tears of the Creator at the creation of Adam, who experiences hardships 'like strong wind' and from whose temple of the body must be driven filth and illicit desires. The second part focuses on the incarnation and the person of Jesus as Redeemer. In this interpretation Jesus weeps over the old law and cleanses the old temple building of old meanings in order to give new meaning to Scripture. The third portion is the drama of the conversion of the individual sinner. Jesus and the Holy Spirit weep with lamentations that the human does not see the dangers. The Spirit remonstrates: 'If only you had recognised the dangers, you would press yourself like a wine press, and like a mill, you would turn yourself here and there'. Because of the temptations of the devil the heart was formerly a brothel; now the 'reddening light' of repentance will descend upon it. Both Gregory the Great and the scholarly monk Bede (672/3–689) render a moral and not a spiritual interpretation of this passage, which bears out the word of the Lord given to Hildegard that she would serve as his writer to declare new mysteries and to reveal secrets hidden in books.

Hildegard describes the help given by the Holy Spirit to the ancient prophets: 'These were the miracles of the Divinity that God brought forth in wondrous ways through the prophets when they spoke, foreseeing what they foresaw in the Spirit, writing what they handed down from memory by command of God, and playing a lyre'.[28] In a similar manner Hildegard's poetry and song are an expression of the prophetic Spirit. Her composition and orchestration of the numerous antiphons, sequences and hymns (collected in the *Symphonia or Symphony of the Harmony of Celestial Revelations)* for her trained choristers are an announcement of the age-old shadows of Christ by prophetic forerunners. These new arrangements anointed by the Spirit are received as fresh revelation by the choir and congregation. By the use of allegorical imagery in the following song, Hildegard engenders vitality and perhaps the desire for a similar wide-eyed prophetic farsightedness today in the reader or singer.

Antiphon for Patriarchs and Prophets 31[29]
Seers in the Former Testament times are sharp-eyed foretellers who reflected, as in a mirror, the vision of God before it came to pass. They understood the shadow, the chiaroscuro (lights and shades) of divine revelation. The Old foreshadows the New; the Old Testament is the root for the shoot of the New Testament:

> O clear-sighted men
> who have pierced secrets,
> seeing with the Spirit's eyes
> and announcing in transparent shadow
> a sharp and living light
> budding on a slender green branch
> and flowered alone,
> taking root from the entry of the light.

The song describes 'clear-sighted' prophets gifted with supernatural foresight who have penetrated mysteries, 'pierced secrets', hidden and only divinely perceived with the 'eyes of the Spirit'. They are empowered to declare in advance, 'in transparent shadow', the truth of the Incarnation, described as 'a sharp and living light'. The new shoot of truth grows (and glows) on the 'slender green branch', that is, the revealed truth of the Old Testament. The imagery of root and shoot is echoed in a responsory for patriarchs and prophets; the old sinful tree in the garden now becomes the new tree of the cross:

> O flourishing
> roots of the tree of wonders
> (no longer the tree of crimes),

a cascade of dappled shadow
rained on your planting.[30]

Liturgical pieces, new and original works of music sung, chanted, read or performed are a potential nerve centre for the display
of prophetic utterance, as the divine drama is spoken or sung not
simply as a past episode but as a present reality. Discerning
Christ as the higher meaning of Scripture is dependent both on
the action of the Spirit in the text and on the prophetic gift given
to Hildegard by Christ (cf. Eph. 4:8,11). Thus there is a unity of
Word and Spirit in both text and prophet.

Outward and inward realities

For Hildegard all temporal and spiritual realities are narrated
and ordered in the prophetical way. The text of Romans 1:20 is
germane to her way of illustrating symbolically the history of
the faith by extensive use of the created order: 'God, who made
all things by his will, created them so that his name would be
known and glorified, showing in them not just the things that
are visible and temporal, but also the things that are invisible
and eternal'.[31]

An example of this principle may be found in the use
Hildegard makes of animal imagery to address the clash between
emperor and pope. In a letter to Eugenius III at the height of the
investiture conflict (the battle between spiritual and temporal
power), she presents the bear and the eagle, personifying emper-
or and pope, respectively, engaged in a struggle for the jewel in
the road, that is, the power of ecclesiastical privilege. She encour-
ages the pope to strengthen his resistance to clerical high living
and to assert his supremacy over the emperor as 'the eagle who
overcomes the bear'. She implores him: 'Do not destroy the sight
of the eye, nor cut off light from light'.[32]

On the landmark occasion when Hildegard enters the political
arena in her eightieth year for the final time, her text is Psalm 150,
'These words use outward, visible things to teach us about
inward things'. The letter to the Prelates of Mainz concerns the
importance of the music of heaven and is an example of the relationship between the outward reality of an unjust church situation and the inward reality of Scripture.[33]

Letter 23

Hildegard writes her defence, her objection to an injustice, the interdict imposed on her community because of their decision to welcome a dying man, excommunicated from the church, absolve him and bury him in the consecrated ground of the convent. The interdict forbade the singing of the Divine Office and participation in the Mass. Hildegard declares the priority of the Spirit in song: 'When we consider these things carefully, we recall that man needed the voice of the living Spirit'. By means of the construction of instruments and the composition of psalms 'these holy prophets get beyond the music of this exile and recall to mind that divine melody of praise which Adam, in company with the angels, enjoyed in God before his fall'. The Spirit is invoked as 'prophetic'; the imperative to worship proceeds from him: 'The body is the vestment of the spirit, which has a living voice, and so it is proper for the body, in harmony with the soul, to use its voice to sing praises to God. Whence in metaphor, the prophetic Spirit commands us to praise God with clashing cymbals and cymbals of jubilation [Ps. 150.5]'. Under pain of excommunication herself, Hildegard ironically informs the clergy that unless they repent they themselves will be exiled from heaven, for preventing the proper praises of God: 'Therefore, those who, without just cause, impose silence on a church and prohibit the singing of God's praises . . . will lose their place among the chorus of angels'. This prophetic stance on the priority of worship did not alter the situation immediately, but the interdict was lifted a few months prior to her death.

Hildegard understands Scripture in the prophetical way as her trained eye searches out the hidden meanings inlaid by the Spirit of God in what she reads. As this is achieved she enters more deeply into imaginative imagery, in order to articulate the meaning of the texts she reads. Her dependence is entirely upon the Spirit to draw out meaning and, as this is pursued, the person of Christ emerges in the text. Word and Spirit work together to disclose prophetical truth. Hildegard's allegorical way is a technique not altogether unfamiliar to Bonhoeffer. The difference between them is that when Hildegard's spontaneous composition is an additional padding to the text it is often lengthy and composed in expansive 'flowery' language. At times one has to seek hard to correlate the text to pertinent issues or concerns. Today we would call it free poetic licence, extemporary writing. Nevertheless her points are made and the evidence for the success of the prophetical way is in the responses from her correspondents to her remarks about character, or warnings, or insights. Bonhoeffer, too, is at pains to expound Scripture in order to draw out the pneumatic or spiritual meaning, but earnestly relates the plain sense at once to the immediate concrete context. Already we have caught a glimpse of his concretization of the text in the circumstances of the church in Germany in the Bible study, 'The Reconstruction of Jerusalem according to Ezra and Nehemiah'. It is this factor which most distances his method from Hildegard. Nevertheless, attentiveness to the passages under examination will show us that there are more commonalities which bind them in their pursuit for right living, than differences which divide them.

Dietrich Bonhoeffer: Reviving the Spiritual Meaning in Scripture

> Scripture is the manger in which Christ is laid (Martin Luther).[34]

We have seen that Bonhoeffer's quest for a word for the historical context in which he lived and theologized puts him at loggerheads with the liberalism of the German academy. He is of the opinion that the very objectivity of revelation has evolved into a science in itself and has very little use for the technique of historical criticism. He wants to underscore the completeness of the biblical revelation as history, hence his acceptance of the historical-critical method only with the proviso that it validates the 'total *historicity* of the revelation'.[35] He contests the weakness in the method in its attention to origins and not to the witness to faith: 'For history, Scripture is only a source; for pneumatology, it is testimony'.[36]

Bonhoeffer's critique of the historical-critical method is expressed in his introduction to the lectures on Genesis (1932/3), in which he makes plain to his students the relationship between the church and biblical authority. He speaks boldly for the biblical

witness: 'We take the Bible into our hands here as the church of
Christ' and 'We must place ourselves under the same Lord under
whom the Bible stands'. His radicalism is provocative: 'one must
read it [the word of God] word for word like a child and learn to
rethink *completely* what the historical critical commentaries teach
us'. His priority is not painstaking textual analysis but 'the text as
it presents itself to the church of Christ today'.[37] If we compare this
primary focus with Hildegard we find that they are not dissimilar.
Both are inherently believers in the divine inspiration of Scripture
and mediated by the Spirit of God for their times.

The treasure is Christ present[38]

For the method of historical-criticism everything depends on the
one doing the interpretation. Scripture is lifeless until the act of
interpretation brings it to life and makes the meaning present.
Bonhoeffer criticizes the 'making present' autonomy over the text
in a talk for the brotherhood of the assistant preachers and curates
of the Confessing Church on 23 August 1935. He fiercely opposes
the task of 'making present' as a human act, as it then becomes the
judge of Scripture. He states that it will lead directly into paganism. He clarifies his point: 'the exposition of texts is not a human
act of "making present", but is always God himself, the Holy
Spirit', and genuine 'making present' is simply the 'making present' of Christ and his word, 'the witness of Christ as the crucified,
resurrected one who summons men into discipleship'. He goes on
to argue for the usefulness of allegorical exposition. If Christ is the
central meaning of Scripture, he is the focus, therefore, of either
literal or allegorical exegesis: 'Why should it not be possible for
the Word to have symbolic or allegorical meaning? The decisive
and single criterion is only whether nothing other than Christ
himself will be discovered here'. He rejoices in the allegorical
exposition of Scripture which is the church's freedom and a cele-
bration of 'the fullness of Christ's witness from Scripture'. He
likens the cutting away and tidying up of irregular and dubious
elements in Scripture to the clipped wings of a wild eagle tamed
and unable to soar.

Like Hildegard, Bonhoeffer makes full use of the 'wild side' of
patristic exegetical practice, extending it to its limits in the service of the church struggle in Germany, especially by his use of

allegory as a weapon against antagonists. His critiques of church and state are jam-packed with the 'types' or 'figures' so often found in church fathers like Origen. Bonhoeffer sees the persons and prophetic utterances in the Old Testament as 'types' and references to the Christ present and speaking even before his advent in New Testament times. Even the literal sense of the text is *not* the historical-factual meaning but the prophetic sense because it points to the coming of Christ. Scripture is assigned a 'more than literal' meaning, a spiritual or pneumatic sense, so that the whole of everyday life has a biblical echo. Christ is the lynchpin which fastens these historical and spiritual realities together. Christ is the subject matter and saving action of both testaments. For Bonhoeffer Christ is the treasure.

If Bonhoeffer's project of the presence of Christ in the Old Testament is untidy and a vexation for those of us who are critical exegetes of the Bible, then we are in good company. His close friend and interpreter, Eberhard Bethge, points out this persistent problem: 'Christ in the Old Testament, to read the Old Testament from Christ, to understand Christ from the Old Testament – that remains to the last'.[39] Controversial or outdated as it may appear, Bonhoeffer's subversion of the text by the use of allegorical types lifts Scripture out of its usual strictures and conventions, so that the reader is surprised (or coerced) into rethinking its entire meaning in light of the current context. In his resolve to bring Christ to the fore, his forceful line of attack may be contrasted with Hildegard's gentler, poetic style. Their intention, however, is the same, i.e. to extract from the text the Christ-figure.

Christ in the Old Testament

Bonhoeffer settles the problem of the unity of the Bible in the notion of the one God of both New and Old Testaments in the concluding notes from the manuscript 'King David': 'The God of the Old Testament is the Father of Jesus Christ. The God of the revealed Jesus Christ is the God of the Old Testament. He is the Trinitarian God'. The Old Testament foreshadows the New Testament: 'The Old Testament must be read in the light of the incarnation and crucifixion, that is, the revelation which has taken place for us. Otherwise we are left with the Jewish or heathen understanding of the Old Testament'.[40]

King David

The three Bible studies, 'King David', delivered in 1935 to curates
of the Confessing Church, were politically explosive. They were
intended as prophetic, even messianic comment on the situation
of anti-Semitism in Germany. Throughout the studies the idea of
David as messianic 'type' is developed; the one who is anointed,
persecuted and identified both with the Jewish race and with the
Confessing Church. David is a pattern or prototype, a 'personal
type of Christ', a 'model' or 'example', and 'shadow', cf. Hebrews
8:5; 10:1. The incarnation holds the key to David as type of Christ:
'David is the shadow of the Messiah become flesh. The shadow
of the incarnation falls on David. As a result the incarnation is
understood as the origin. By the will of the incarnation and from
the incarnation David is the messianic king'. In the first study,
'The Anointing and Persecution of David', the same Spirit
anoints both David and Christ: 'The Spirit of anointing is the
Spirit of the messianic kingship. It is the one Spirit of God, with
which David was anointed, and Christ (Lk. 4:18)'. The presence
of Christ is strongly in David to defeat Goliath: 'as the one anointed for the messianic kingdom as model and shadow of Christ,
David was victorious over Goliath. This is the victory of Christ in
him. Because Christ was in David'. By implication there is the
assurance of victory for the Confessing Church because Christ is
in it.

The second study, 'The Messianic King', asserts God's prophetic purposes both for the Jewish people, in the text, 'Who is like
your people, like Israel?' (2 Sam. 7:23), and the church, in the
cleansing of the temple. Bonhoeffer states publicly, 'The people of
Israel will remain God's people eternally, the only people that
will not disappear, because God has become its Lord, God has
taken residence in them and built his house. The church, the true
Israel, is promised'. Bonhoeffer's inflammatory remarks, that the
Jews were God's 'chosen people', the 'true noble race', 'God's
people', are called 'audacious' by the SS journalist, Friedrich
Imholz, on 26 March 1936, in the newspaper *Durchbruch*.[14]

The third study, 'David, the Justified Sinner' (2 Sam. 11 – 19),
strikes another provocative prophetic chord. Christ and his
church (signified by David and his seed) are struck by the violence
of the sword but the promise is not destroyed. Godly punishment

(symbolized by the sword) against the church (the house of David) reinstates the promise. The church under the cross (the crucified Christ) arises to receive new life. The study becomes more subversive with the German Christians (Absalom's revolt) pitted against the Confessing Church (the house of David). However, the self-judgement and ruin of Absalom in contrast with God's judgement on David by the sword is a consoling promise for the war-weary pastors of the Confessing Church.

Christ in the Psalms[42]

If the notes on 'King David' are unpalatable to our sanitized reading of the Bible, we are faced with another embarrassing hurdle in Bonhoeffer's view of Jesus in the Psalms. He rejects the historical-critical method in the notes for the lecture, 'Christ in the Psalms', given on 31 July 1935 to the Pomeranian students of the Confessing Church. He contends that the outcome of this discussion will affect the whole future of theological interpretation as it is dependent on the acceptance either of the dogmatic thesis of verbal inspiration or textual criticism. The notes hinge on the problem of the 'I', the identity of the speaker or petitioner in the psalms.

Bonhoeffer advocates a return to the orthodox way of viewing the 'I' in the psalms as 'the voice of Christ within his Old Testament community' and to which faith the psalms testify. He states that 'the orthodox position wanted to make God visible . . . in the verbal inspiration of the Bible'. The conclusion to the lecture is briefly annotated in cryptic format in an editorial revision of Bonhoeffer's notes in a series of statements about Christ's presence in the psalms: 'Christ as the predicted, Christ as the promise, the faithfulness of God, as the Word. Christ as the one who is believed in. Christ as the accused . . . In Christ as the Crucified: 1. as one destined for the cross by God, 2. as one accused by the people through piety and impiety'. Christ embodies the fullness of revelation, and Bonhoeffer seeks to maintain its completeness by permitting the 'I' in the psalms to embrace all of human motive, both the good and the evil. He takes this premise to an extreme in the 'psalms of cursing', where the cries for justice against enemies come from the mouth of Christ. These notions are not easy to swallow, as they challenge our comfortable scrubbing of the

uncomfortable words in the Old Testament, particularly in contexts where inhumane injustices lead very often to a cul de sac
with no apparent hope of forgiveness.

Christ in the cursing psalms[43]
Bonhoeffer's awkward and controversial rendering of Christ and
the cursing psalms must be seen in the context of the unjust
imprisonment of members of the Confessing Church and his own
house arrest. The Meditation on Psalm 58 during a seminar in
Finkenwalde in 1937 expresses Bonhoeffer's conviction that
Christians are able to pray the angry psalms because Christ prays
them. Christ 'accuses the godless, he calls down upon them
God's vengeance and justice'. Christ cries out words of condem-
nation as our representative, our deputy, as *Stellvertretung*, as
'one who steps into our place', as one who participates in our
cries of pain and identifies with the human plight in all its evil
intent. Thus Bonhoeffer can assert with utter confidence that 'in
the midst of this distress Christ prays this psalm vicariously as
our representative'. In calling down God's wrath he is invoking
it *upon himself*, praying that God's vengeance be taken on his own
body as the substitute for sin, and, leaving justice in the hands of
God, 'he gives himself for the benefit of all the godless with his
innocent suffering on the cross'. Therefore every human curse,
every vindictive thought or action, and every prayer leads to the
crucified Christ. This unbelievable complexity, this affront to our
sensibilities that Christ identifies with suffering humanity to that
sort of limit, is traceable in the tradition with which Bonhoeffer
was familiar, and summed up in the word *Anfechtung*, anxiety, or
trials and temptations. The idea of *Anfechtung* rescues the offence
of Christ's vicarious action and places it firmly as a psychologically valid solution for our overburdened and stressful lives.

Anfechtung
We know that Bonhoeffer grappled with the same state of
Anfechtung as did Augustine, because he had in his possession a
copy of Augustine's commentary on the psalms, translated as
Über die Psalmen, in which numerous passages were underlined,
including verses from Psalm 118 (119). That Augustine is anxious
about the state of his own soul and those of the heathen is evident

in his comment on Psalm 119:19 (1), 'I am a sojourner upon earth; O hide not Thy commandments from me'. His absorption with the differences between 'those whose conversation is in heaven' and those preoccupied with earthly affairs is that they are 'in truth strangers'. He is immensely concerned 'that the commandments of God may not be hidden from them'.[44] Strands of Augustinian *Anfechtung* plague Bonhoeffer: 'That God might sometimes hide God's own command from me (Ps. 119:19), that God may someday not let me recognize the divine will, is the deepest anxiety [*Anfechtung*] of the new life'.[45] Bonhoeffer's troubled thoughts find solace in the psalms where God takes the full weight of human tribulation. In the psalms there are answers for the struggling anxiety-ridden believer:

> There is no theoretical answer to all these questions in the psalms any more than in the New Testament. The only real answer is Jesus Christ. But this answer is already being sought in the psalms. It is common to all of them that they cast every difficulty and tribulation [*Anfechtung*] upon God: 'We can no longer bear them, take them away from us and bear them yourself, for you alone can handle suffering'.[46]

Scripture in community

The difficulties and dilemmas of the problem of *Anfechtung* lead Bonhoeffer to community. For him God alone is never sufficient. It is always God in community by means of his living word. The solution to the problem of *Anfechtung* is community plus the Bible. He asks, 'How are we supposed to help rightly other Christians who are experiencing troubles and temptation [*Anfechtung*] if not with God's own word?'[47] In the place of *Anfechtung* and inner turmoil someone brings strengthening relief in a word they have found to be profound: 'When the heart is weak and uncertain the living word is brought by a person who has been struck by it and our hunger is fed'.[48] The site for the disclosure of truth is community, not Christians in isolation. In times of the very real predicaments of stress and anxiety Bonhoeffer returns to the Bible in community as a pillar of power. In his commentary on the Psalter, *Prayerbook of the Bible*, he introduces the indwelling Christ who prays within the individual and in and through the community of faith: 'It is important for us that even David prayed not only out of the personal ruptures of his heart, but from the Christ dwelling in him. To be sure, the one who prays these psalms, David, remains himself; but Christ dwells in him and with him'.[49] Christ in us, Christ in community is Bonhoeffer's mantra. To pray the psalms is to pray with Christ:

> Who prays the Psalter? David (Solomon, Asaph, etc.) prays. Christ prays. We pray. We who pray are, first of all, the whole community of faith in which alone the entire richness of the Psalter can be prayed. But those who pray are also, finally, all individuals insofar as they have a part in Christ and in their congregation and share in the praying of their prayer.[50]

Bonhoeffer's introduction of the mostly forgotten monastic discipline of psalmody into the experimental Finkenwalde seminary inspires togetherness as community. Meditation and profound reflection in a communal setting help banish the cries of *Anfechtung*. Antiphonal singing of psalms (the exercise of chant or song in alternative verses or strophes from side to side of the church or choir) unifies the members of the community. The single petitioner can never be alone but is always linked to another through the person of the praying Christ: 'The one who prays never prays alone. There must always be a second person, another, a member of the church, the body of Christ, indeed Jesus Christ himself, praying with the Christian in order that the prayer of the individual may be true prayer'.[51] Bonhoeffer's Finkenwalde community is joined with Christ and one another through the Bible in a dynamic circle of fellowship.

Bonhoeffer commends Hebraic parallelism (two parts of a verse emphasizing the same thought) as an aid to antiphonal and communal singing: 'It invites us to pray together with one another . . . So the verse form specifically summons us to pray the psalms together'.[52] The built-in pause, the *selah*, allows time for the inspiration of the Spirit; here he refers to Martin Luther (1483–1546): '"The *selah* indicates that one must be still and quickly reflect on the words of the psalm; for they demand a quiet and restful soul, which can grasp and hold to that which the Holy Spirit there presents and offers"'.[53] In this quiet meditation on a portion of Scripture we receive something quite personal: 'We expose ourselves to the particular sentence and word until we personally are affected by it'.[54] An extract from a letter on 8 April 1936, to Dr Rüdiger Schleicher, commends meditative reading as an act of inward reflection:

> When a dear friend speaks a word to us, do we subject it to analysis? No, we simply accept it, and then it resonates inside us for days. The word of someone we love opens itself up to us the more we 'ponder it in our hearts', as Mary did. In the same way we should carry the Word of the Bible around with us. We will only be happy in our reading of the Bible when we dare to approach it as the means by which God really speaks to us, the God who loves us and will not leave us with our questions unanswered.[55]

Bonhoeffer's communal reading of the psalms is modelled on the monastic pattern, and the resemblances to Hildegard's Benedictine way are straightforward. The difference is that in Finkenwalde the brothers were openly accountable to each other as they prayed together without the constraints of the liturgy. Similarly today an approach to one another in mutual confidentiality is a particular hallmark of pastoral care. This would not have been the practice in Hildegard's community. Confession of sin was indeed the convention of the day but as a practice within the sacrament of confession with a confessor.

Countercultural reading

The monastic practice of *lectio divina* (sacred reading) introduced into the Finkenwalde community reflects Bonhoeffer's own spiritual discipline, as the evidence of two texts reveals. These examples show us that Bonhoeffer read actively, with his heart on the passage and his mind on Germany. His response to the Crystal Night pogrom of the burning of synagogues is to mark Psalm 74:8, 'they burned all the meeting-places of God in the land', with the date, 9 November 1938, in the Bible he used for meditation, and to place an exclamation mark next to the following verse:

> We do not see our emblems;
>   there is no longer any prophet,
>   and there is none among us who knows how long.[56]

The resolution of Bonhoeffer's dilemma in the Prophet's Chamber (a room set apart for visiting lecturers to Union Seminary, USA), to return to Germany, having only arrived on 2 June 1939, is undergirded by Scripture, as is recorded in his diary, 20 June 1939. He understands the readings for that day, Isaiah 45:19 and 1 Peter 1:17, in light of his resolve. We note the element of *Anfechtung* and the plea for God's mercy when there is little light:

> Today the reading speaks dreadfully harshly of God's incorruptible judgment. He certainly sees how much personal feeling, how much anxiety there is in today's decision, however brave it may seem. The reasons one gives for an action to others and to one's self are certainly inadequate. One can give a reason for everything. In the last resort one acts from a level which remains hidden from us. So one can only ask God to judge us and to forgive us.[57]

The 1732 publication of *Hernhuter Lösungen* was a collection of brief texts forming the daily devotional for a pious German which Bonhoeffer was accustomed to read. The *Lösung* for 26 June based on the text, 2 Timothy 4:21, 'Do your best to come before winter', spurs him on in his determination to go back to stand with his fellow countrymen in the Confessing Church in its desperate hour of need.[58] It is significant that this decision to return to his homeland led to Bonhoeffer's arrest and exile from those he loved. Nevertheless his love for Scripture remains and his familiar practice of meditation is a comfort to him in prison: 'Before I go to sleep I repeat to myself the verses that I have learnt during the day, and at 6 a.m. I like to read the psalms and hymns'.[59]

Bonhoeffer's contribution to the prophetic enterprise of discerning the times in Scripture is in his recovery of the historic and pneumatic realities from patristic exegesis and in the restoration of the practice of the *lectio divina*. It has been shown that when the hermeneutical circle of the community of faith is in harmony with Christ as interpreter of Scripture the word of the Lord breaks through clearly and decisively. His method of engaging with the dual realities of biblical text and context through the idea of the 'presence of Christ' brings about at times a painful conflict with the prevailing culture. He stands back to take a hard look and to hear the cries (Jer. 8:7,22; 9:1; 31:15). It may well be that in turning to the Old Testament to bear the brunt of his protest, particularly to the person of Christ within it, he sees himself as a 'type' of Christ, identifying with the pain in the text and bearing it vicariously on behalf of those for whom he prays.

Reading the Signs of the Times through Scripture

We are overwhelmed by the big picture Bonhoeffer paints of the person of Jesus Christ. That figure fills the canvas, edge to edge. With utter conviction and humanist energy, the artist's portrayal is of the God-man, the go-between, the Man for others, to whom our allegiance must be given, despite political or personal pressure. Bonhoeffer is a model to emulate as we are fascinated by his own struggle with Scripture and the outcomes it presents for our lives. Hildegard sets down her theology more often than not in an unusual style and obscure imagery. She is not as persuasive as Bonhoeffer in the application of the text to the everyday; her devotional style differs from his pragmatic approach. Nevertheless, Jesus Christ is presented as the nucleus of the times and seasons. As we have seen, both writers determine the spiritual meaning in their worlds by the regular practice of meditative reflection upon portions of Scripture. Although the plain sense or the literal explanation is a first concern, the method of *lectio divina* fosters an involvement with the higher meaning – wrestling with the underlying prophetic or pneumatic sense. Bonhoeffer refuses the abstractions of the academy in his default position, which is always Christ, in the concrete circumstances of his day. For both theologians Christ is the fulcrum and, as they read, it is as though the Holy Spirit triggers the detonation of biblical texts which, like time bombs, explode into their times at just the right moment, charged with life-giving power.

From these ponderings we may glean a specific route to follow in our desire to see and to hear the word of Christ today. If we are to acquire the nuggets of truth, the revelation available for each day, every Sunday, every life situation, then the ancient path of the prophetical way is a good route forward. This will mean finding time in my busy schedule as a leader to sit before the Lord of the Scriptures, at his footstool as it were, with the Bible on my lap, to invite or invoke the Holy Spirit to uncover Christ the Word, to point the way in my life. This personal revelation may well become the word to read the signs to inspire and teach others.

3.

COMMUNITY OF VISION

Better two than one alone, since thus their work is really reward-
ing. If one should fall, the other helps him up; but what of the person with no one to help him up when he falls? Again: if two sleep
together they keep warm, but how can anyone keep warm alone?
Where one alone would be overcome, two will put up resistance;
and a threefold cord is not quickly broken (Eccl. 4:9–12, The New
Jerusalem Bible).

The Social Network

The divine-human encounter is epitomized in the biblical story of
Jacob's struggle with the angel (or God). It concludes with the
strike against Jacob's hip and a leader who walks thereafter with
a limp (Gen. 32:22–32). Is this the fable of everyman who contends with God and prevails? Is it the triumph of a sovereign God
over and against rebellious humanity? The wounding of Jacob is
a parable of one-in-community. It is a tiny tale of one responsible
father, husband and brother, yet one whose family is given over
for a night to make way for the greater narrative of one held in
relationship with his God. Does Jacob's battle prefigure another
in the garden of Gethsemane? Jesus Christ kneels as a wounded
struggler surrendered to a greater control on behalf of an ultimate
destiny. Jesus Christ as truly God (*verus Deus*) and truly man
(*verus homo*) is the predicament of the paradoxical God-man.

As Christians we know that we belong *both* to the human family *and* to God and we are impaled at times on the horns of a
dilemma of dual loyalties. The writings of Hildegard and

Bonhoeffer illustrate this conflict and together help to overcome it. The piety of Hildegard is governed by the medieval expression of devotion to Christ generated by the desire for heaven. The dedication of Bonhoeffer is a discipleship of ethical courage and perseverance in the face of the dark night on earth. In this work we are concerned to find a synergy between the testimony to the person of Christ in glory *and* the suffering Jesus in the world in order to activate balanced and rounded prophecy.

It would be unproblematic for us to assume that strategies for the implementation of Hildegard's projects came only from the help and support of her powerful friends and family. This suits our notion of community far better than the acceptance that her initial turn as prophet is to the influence of the Living Light. Her vision, however, is lodged outside of the world as we know it and her appeal is, firstly, to the community of the Trinity upon whose wisdom she entirely depends. Her theological angle on Jesus is 'truly God' but is mysteriously portrayed at one and the same time as the human figure within the cosmic Trinity. The dictates of Bonhoeffer's conscience and his theological strivings are determined well within the boundaries of the concrete family of humanity. His absorption with 'this-worldliness' upholds the community of real personhood and identification with the suffering of the 'other'. Jesus as 'truly man' is the dominant aspect; its potency is the withstanding of human solitariness by means of the community of Christ our brother.

Imago Dei

De Lubac addresses the question of personhood by extensive use of patristic and medieval literature, in order to counter the idea that religion is privatized and individualistic, and to argue for the social nature of Christianity. His discourse on the threefold relationship of the Trinity is the starting point for a wonderfully complete expression of personality and unity. The vocation of a single person is to become an integral part of the spiritual body of Christ in the likeness of the Trinity, and to enter upon relationships with others where there is no solitary state.[1]

De Lubac identifies the annihilation of the human person as one of the consequences of the rejection of God. Absolute humanism is the drive to eliminate God and to exalt the human being, and is the result of the drift away from the central patristic-medieval tenet of the image of God (*imago Dei*) in Genesis 1:26.[2] De Lubac abandons proofs for the existence of God and emphasizes the original divine–human encounter. The discovery of God is a return to source, to God's initiative in making himself known, and this is completely possible because we are made in his image and have 'the mark of God upon us'.[3] He argues that the incarnation of the Son of God has made it possible for all to become children of God by the illumination of the Spirit. He contends for deification because of the imprint of the image of God in every soul.[4] De Lubac promotes a return to a central tenet of patristic theology, first enunciated by Athanasius (d.373), the notion of *theosis*, i.e. deification, divinization, or making divine of human beings: 'For he was made man that we might be made God'.

Hands of God

Three main doctrines of the church father Irenaeus (120–202) became part of the early Trinitarian confession as a rule of faith and are still sound tenets today. He formulated the threefold cord of God the Father as Creator of the universe, the Word as the Son bringing communion and peace with God, and the Holy Spirit re-creating human beings for God. This early doctrinal rule underpins Hildegard's grasp of an economic Trinity, i.e. one which stresses the functions of each person in the management of the created order. So that we may better pinpoint the workings of Word and Spirit and their joint co-operation in creative prophecy in both Hildegard and Bonhoeffer, we turn to Irenaeus and his compact bodily image of two hands. To decipher the puzzling image of two hands, two executors, is to see that they signify Christ the Word and the Holy Spirit active together from the beginning in the creative and saving purposes of God. God's divine grip on the world is, and always has been, two-handed. This is a biblical code which helps us to listen for echoes between the view of the Trinity in the church fathers, medieval interpretation in Hildegard, and Bonhoeffer's reformed tradition.

In Irenaeus' treatise 'Against Heresies', the inner dialogue of the Trinity, 'Let us make man', initiates the creation of Adam, 'moulded by his hands, that is, by the Son and Holy Spirit' (Gen. 1:26). God moves as one: 'For with him were always present the

Word and Wisdom, the Son and the Spirit'.[5] The movement of
both hands in concert sculpts and lifts up the bodies of Elijah and
Enoch (2 Kgs 2:11; Gen. 5:24, cf. Heb. 11:5): 'For, by means of the
very same hands through which they were moulded at the beginning, did they receive this translation and assumption. For in
Adam the hands of God had become accustomed to set in order,
to rule, and to sustain His own workmanship, and to bring it and
place it where they pleased.'[6]

Irenaeus wishes to underscore the power of God in the most
impossible of situations (cf. Luke 18:27). The exegesis of Daniel
3:19–25 underlines the rescue operation performed by the divine
strong hand: 'from the fiery furnace men issued forth unhurt, yet
they nevertheless did so, led forth as it were by the hand of God,
for the purpose of declaring his power'.[7] The pre-existent Creator
Christ, who shaped the human being at the beginning of all
things, is the incarnate hand of God on earth, present to heal and
to save (John 9:6):

> He gave sight, not by means of a word, but by an outward action
> . . . Wherefore also the Lord spat on the ground and made clay, and
> smeared it upon the eyes, pointing out the original fashioning [of
> man], how it was effected, and manifesting the hand of God to
> those who can understand by what [hand] man was formed out of
> the dust . . . knowing that this hand of God which formed us at the
> beginning, and which does form us in the womb, has in the last
> times sought us out who were lost.[8]

From the image of the two hands of God in Irenaeus can be
deduced the principle of their co-operation in the inner working
of the gift of prophecy, with which the present study is concerned. Two key biblical texts show the operations of both Christ
and the Spirit in prophetic utterance. Read together, they establish not only the necessary presence, but also the intrinsic unity
of Christ and the Spirit in prophecy. The first text shows that the
person of Christ, the divine Word, is the prophetic impulse itself
within the word of the prophet: 'For the testimony of Jesus is the
Spirit of prophecy' (Rev. 19:10d). Justin Martyr (d.c.165) explains
that 'when you hear the phrases of the prophets spoken as
though from a character, do not suppose that they were spoken

as from the inspired ones themselves, but rather from the divine Logos [Word] moving them'.[9] The second text firmly secures the prophetic gift to the Holy Spirit: 'First of all you must understand this, that no prophecy of Scripture is a matter of one's own inter-pretation, because no prophecy ever came by human will, but men and women moved by the Holy Spirit spoke from God' (2 Pet. 1:20–21). The first text is discussed in the present chapter in relation to prophecy as a testimony to Jesus Christ; the second, on the role of the Spirit is examined in Chapter 4.

The Person of Jesus Christ

The phrase, 'the testimony of Jesus', is multi-layered in its inter-pretation. It could be understood to mean 'the testimony borne by Jesus' or maintained by the historical Jesus, as in Revelation 1:5 and 5:5 (cf. Matt. 27:11–14; Mark 15:1–5; Luke 23:1–12; John 18:19–24,33–38). The stronger reading understands the phrase 'the testimony of Jesus' ('*hē gar martyria Iēsou*') as an objective genitive, 'the testimony of or about Jesus', which refers to the wit-ness to Christ which all believers bear and not only those desig-nated prophets. An exegesis of the enigmatic phrase 'the Spirit of prophecy' ('*to pneuma tēs prophēteias*') renders the obvious inter-pretation that 'testifying about Jesus is the heart of prophecy'. A translation, however, which lays the emphasis on the possessive case stresses the activity of the Holy Spirit and induces the mean-ing, 'Spirit-inspired prophecy'. Here the critical link is made between the Spirit, the bearer of prophecy, and Jesus Christ, the witness of prophecy. In Jewish tradition the phrase, 'the Spirit of prophecy', is a favourite name and a regular rabbinic term for the Spirit of God. Joseph, for example, is one in whom is found the Spirit of God (Gen. 41:38), meaning the ability to interpret dreams, and one who, in respect of general wisdom, manifests 'the prophetic spirit'. This reading is consistent with the revela-tion of Jesus Christ in other significant texts: John 15:26; Acts 16:7; 1 Peter 1:11. The general witness of the New Testament is that 'the Spirit of prophecy is the Spirit of Jesus'.[10]

For the shape of prophetic utterance, therefore, the person of Jesus Christ is of primary importance. In the 1948 Bampton

Lectures, Austin Farrer pinpoints the fusion between the prophet, Christ and the Spirit. Prophets are those who 'simply had their minds charged with the word of God'. John, the poet, was a prophet writing his apocalypse, receiving confirmation from his familiar angel and saying in effect, 'I am a fellow-servant . . . with thee, and with thy brethren that have the testimony of Jesus; for the testimony of Jesus is the spirit of your prophecy' [Rev. 19:10].[11]

In Hildegard the doctrine of the person and work of Jesus Christ is of utmost importance. Her *visio* encompasses the full gamut of the revelation of the Son as pre-existent, incarnate and judge at the end of the age. At the very core of her theology lies the mystery of the incarnation as the final cause of creation. The accent on redemption in the opening lines of *Scivias* and the suffering of Christ is shared with much of the writing of the medieval period. More than this, however, is the fact that the cosmic visions in *Scivias* reveal a very human Jesus. The figure of a man in the midst of the whirring cosmic imagery of the Trinity, so common to Hildegard, is food for thought. As Dronke points out, 'the human is inseparable from the divine . . . in truth [the human] is at the centre of the divine'.[12] The person of Christ as the human factor within the divine is a significant part of Hildegard's *visio* and is at the heart of this discussion of the Trinity as community.

Hildegard of Bingen: Cosmic Community of Light

> For with you is the fountain of life;
>   in your light we see light (Ps. 36:9).

We may understand the word *visio* (vision) in two respects: firstly, it is the visionary gift itself; secondly, it is the specific paranormal elements – the vision or revelation – of what is heard and seen. Hildegard's *visio*, the prophetic gift itself, is given to the seer to enable her to see the things of God. Hildegard is enmeshed in an environment particularly appropriate for a vision of heavenly matters. A new spiritual impulse in the Benedictine way, inspired by Anselm (1033–1109), brought a different dimension. He advocated a withdrawal into a kind of hermitage of the mind in order to draw closer to God in a fervent, intimate relationship, leading over time into the visionary experience.[13] The interjection of the supernatural upon her in the impact of her fiery stream of inspiration is precisely the key given by the Spirit to unlock the door to teleology, to the long view of things, to heaven itself, to infinity and to eternity.

Pure light

We know that physical sight is impeded by a blackout. A very old trend in the spiritual tradition, *via negativa* (the way of negation), emphasizes the goodness and purity of darkness, where God is best comprehended. Those who struggle with this accepted wisdom will rejoice that Hildegard is not of that ilk, and that, on the contrary, her expression of the ineffable is always exuberant and never negative. How can it be when her *visio* is the product of the Shade of the Living Light? For Hildegard God is present where there is light: 'Now if luminosity is without darkness, it is called pure light. The light is a living eye, but blindness is at work in the darkness . . . [I]n the light we behold God's works, and in the darkness God's absence'.[14] Her cosmic perspective reflects one of the philosophies of the nature and propagation of light and colour in medieval optics, i.e. rays of light reflected from the object and sent to the observer. For example, in the song 'Sequence for Saint Maximin', marvellous divine light infiltrates the saint's cell to illuminate his ignorance:

> The heat of the sun blazed out
> to irradiate the dark (v. 1b).

Light as a source of divine vision is assimilated with the impetus of the flight of the eagle to convey Maximin's heavenly desires for the greater view: 'he who longed for an eagle's wings' (v. 3b). The eagle is marked out by wings set alight at a height by the divine sun. Likewise the saint newly made luminous, *'lucent Maximin'*, arises with quickened human aspiration to pray for the community of seekers, for those 'who strive toward the mirror/of light' (v. 5).[15] This turn of phrase intimates the medieval view of mirror (*speculum*) for the reflection of divine and human objects, and conjures up a feeling of comprehension which is utterly free of distortion. This is the sense in 'Antiphon for St John the Evangelist', where John is addressed as 'mirror of the dove'. In the 'Sequence for the Holy Spirit', the Spirit is addressed as 'limpid mirror of God'.[16]

One life in three energies

> She caught the crying of those Three,
> The Immortals of the eternal ring,
> Utterer, Utterèd, Uttering.[17]

Lines from an English poet, Gerard Manley Hopkins (1844–89), read like an echo of Hildegard's *visio* of the Trinity: the Father as the Speaker (Creator), the Son as the Spoken (Word) and the Spirit as the Speaking (creative words) in a communicating circle. The 'eternal ring' summarizes the notion of 'inseparability' which distinguishes the patristic-medieval idea of the Trinity: 'What One does All do'.[18] Augustine writes on the Trinity: 'But I do assert with absolute confidence that the Father, the Son, and the Holy Spirit, being of one and the same substance, God the Creator, the omnipotent Trinity, work together inseparably'.[19]

Hildegard conforms in every respect to the convention of 'inseparability' in the Trinity: 'because the Father is not without the Son, nor the Son without the Father, nor the Father or the Son without the Holy Spirit, nor the Holy Spirit without them'.[20] Nevertheless her extensive use of cosmic hyperbole puts the Trinity in a class of its own. The Trinity is a cosmic powerhouse, a combusting dynamic, a combined elemental force field of 'one life in three energies'.[21]

The theological problems with which the medieval period grappled may seem eccentric to our ears, bewildering and unimportant minuscule issues. Here is an example of the Trinitarian problem which is put to Hildegard by Eberhard, bishop of Bamberg, 'since you are imbued by the Holy Spirit'. It evokes a response which energetically confirms the True Light to be the source indeed of her intelligence, enabling her stoutly to refute a numerical doctrine of the Trinity. In her letter to the bishop she graphically portrays a vibrant and colourful vision of the Trinity, which contests with ease the dry formulae of the medieval Schoolmen. The Father is *'eternitas'* (eternity), the Son is *'equalitas'* (equality) and the Spirit is *'connexio'* (an organic binding together, a close union). By means of sustained cosmological allegory Hildegard reconstructs Augustine's early mathematical equation that 'unity is in the Father, equality is in the Son, the harmony of unity and equality is in the Spirit'.[22]

Eternal wheel[23]
In the image we come face to face with the strange and the mysterious in Hildegard's attempt to capture the inexpressible by means of a picture drawn from the everyday. The Trinity is shown as a wheel, completely perfect and ceaselessly in motion. The Father is 'eternity', a circular, rounded action without beginning or end, addition or subtraction: 'Eternity is and always has been. What is eternity? It is God. For eternity is not eternity except in perfect life. Therefore, God lives in eternity'. 'Eternity' is the concern with a quality of life integral to matter. 'Eternity' is related to paternity, to the uncreated Father and origin of all things, in contrast with Lucifer, the symbol of the 'nothing' of 'insolent pride'. In the scientific work, *Causae et Curae*, the fall of Lucifer is compared with the fullness of God, who 'remained complete like a wheel'.[24] In the same work Hildegard asserts the sovereignty of paternity in relation to a wheel: 'Thus paternity is the circle of a wheel. How? Paternity is the fullness of a wheel. It is divinity in itself and all things are from it and there is no creator apart from it'.[25]

The image of the wheel is found elsewhere in the corpus with scriptural echoes to denote divine and human movement. The vision of the cosmic wheel in *Divine Works* is an exegesis of Genesis 1 – 3. The vast universal turning wheel is a fiery force which embraces the human form, who stands in its hub with outstretched arms and is larger than the sphere of the earth. The wheel is driven by winds and animal impulses which keep all things in restless motion and the human being bound to their power.[26] In *Scivias* the wheel represents the human being, foolish if he looks to himself and not to the Creator, 'to the one who tirelessly spins the wheel of his body'.[27] The song, 'To the Virgins', lauds those who look to their Creator and whose 'clear serenity shines in the Wheel of Godhead'.[28] Forth-tellers, prophets and patriarchs mirror the divine wheel in their speech: 'Like wheels you/spun round in wonder as you spoke'.[29] In a song the same vivid wheel image used to depict the Father is used of the Son to stress the idea of 'equality':

> O Word of the Father,
> You are the light of the first dawn
> In the sphere of the circle;
> And You were active
> Like a wheel
> Which encircles all things
> And has neither beginning nor end.[30]

Tunic of equality

In Letter 31r the relationship between the Father as 'eternity' and the Son as 'equality' is formulated allegorically by means of the 'tunic' image. The link between divinity and humanity is made 'tunically' (*tunicaliter*). The shedding of the tunic of equality and the taking up of the tunic of humanity has its source in Philippians 2:5–8:

> [He] did not regard equality with God
> > as something to be exploited . . .
> > being born in human likeness (vv. 6,7).

Hildegard puts it thus: 'Afterward, God humbled himself to his own work, and in this way equality to mankind is an essential quality of the Son of God, for he himself put on the garment of humanity, just as the works of God clothed themselves in their physical forms.'

Elsewhere in her writings Hildegard employs the idea of 'tunic' in diverse ways to paint a poetic picture of God as a divine tailor. In a discussion of the creation in *Divine Works*, God tailor-makes the human race according to 'the tunic of his image', not as an off-the-peg impersonal action, but as an intimate moment, described in *Rewards of Life* thus: 'By loving, [God] embraced it "tunically"'.[31] In the incarnation the Son is undressed, equality with his Father is laid aside, and, in order to convince the world of his equality with it, he is clothed in the tunic of humility (Phil. 2:5–8): 'For the prophetic words shadowed forth his coming, and then appeared fully formed, when the Son of God descended from the lofty mountain, that is, from the heart of his Father, to put on the garment of humanity'.[32] The ultimate dress-down Friday is the final stripping of the Son by crucifixion. Words from Hildegard's song graphically tell the tale of the washing of the old tunic of sin in the blood of the cross:

> And your Word
> Clothed himself in flesh
> In that form
> Which was taken from Adam.
> And thus his garment
> Was cleansed
> By his great pain.[33]

Connection by fire

In Letter 31r the Spirit is the link of fiery love between Father and Son. The image is one of a perpetually burning fire in eternity. The Spirit is likened to a human being who ties up a bundle of disparate parts, the bundle representing the other parts of the godhead, and to a blacksmith who fires two materials, Father and Son, into one. The image of the revolving sword implies that the Spirit is characterized by a burning penetration of God's entirety.

> The connection between eternity and equality is the Holy Spirit. The Holy Spirit is a fire, but it is not an extinguishable fire that sometimes blazes up and sometimes is put out. It permeates eternity and equality, and binds the two into one, just as a person binds together a bundle of sticks (which, if not bound, flies all asunder). And it is like a blacksmith who unites the two materials of bronze and makes them one through fire. It is a sword brandished in every direction. The Holy Spirit reveals eternity and enkindles equality, joining them into one. The Holy Spirit is fire and life in eternity and equality, because God is living.

The drama of salvation history is depicted figuratively in the warlike gladiator in *Rewards of Life*. The action is centred on the unconquerable person of the pre-existent and uncreated Christ, the final judge of all work: 'Who can conquer me? No one! For I have no material in my make-up; no man brought me forth from a woman. But I judge everyone's works'.[34] Whereas Jesus, the Redeemer, is personified as a human being, the essential unity of the Trinity is symbolized by the three cutting edges of the brandished sword in the hand of the gladiator.

The unfolding cosmic imagery in Letter 31r does not present a homely portrait of the Trinity, but a perspicacious kaleidoscope of eternal realities, conceived in multifaceted ideas, each one adding to the whole. What distinguishes Hildegard's doctrine from the Schools is that it is drawn from natural observations of stone, flame, word, sound, breath, light, wheel and person, and the combination of allegorical vision and Scripture are a wellspring of life, energy and power from which surges an unusual form consistent both in its inseparability and redemptive purpose.

The Light of Christ

The visions in *Scivias* II, 2, 5 of three inanimate powers of stone, word and flame are almost, but not quite the same as the representation of light, human being and fire in Scivias II, 2. In this vision the dominance of the human figure of the Son is loudly declared by the one brilliant light in a mutual outpouring, a bathing one over the other, light over fire, fire over light, and light and fire over the human form:

> Then I saw a bright light, and in this light the figure of a man the colour of sapphire, which was all blazing with a gentle glowing fire. And that bright light bathed the whole of the glowing fire, and the glowing fire bathed the bright light; and the bright light and the glowing fire poured over the whole human figure, so that the three were one light in one power of potential.[35]

Light is the central feature in the gleaming sapphire-coloured Christ man, the burning red fire of the Spirit and the clear light of the Father. There are shades of the unchanging Father of lights (Jas 1:17), in whom there is no darkness at all (1 John 1:5), who lives in inaccessible light (1 Tim. 6:16). Hildegard's gloss (interpretation) of the vision explains that the clear light 'depicts the Father without blemish of mocking, weakening or deceit'. The translation of *defectio* as 'weakening' gives the impression of light failing, in the sense of an eclipse and obscuration of the heavenly bodies, and signifies the impossibility of the light of the Father ever going out.[36] The Holy Spirit is a familiar fire (Luke 3:16; Acts 2:3), but the words 'reddish glow' or 'pleasant red fire' add a deeper dimension comparable to the 'prayer of fire' in traditional imagery describing the descent of the Holy Spirit in eastern theology.[37]

The transparent colour blue has strong associations with the humanity of the Son and resonates with the personified virtue, Charity, in the vision of the pillar of the Saviour's humanity in *Scivias*: 'She is a deep sky-blue like a hyacinth, both in person and in tunic; for through his humanity, the incarnate Son of God enlightened faithful and heavenly people, as a hyacinth illumines any object on which it is put down'.[38]

The pattern of redemption in Hildegard corresponds to the medieval concept of the capacity of light to diffuse and to reveal. Examples of this notion may be found in the redemptive visions in *Scivias*, which are a pictorial representation of John 1:5: 'The light shines in the darkness, and the darkness did not overcome it'. Hildegard sees Christ, the Redeemer, engaging the darkness with the weapon of his own radiance. Such is the power of light that it frees the trapped man: 'And I saw a light-filled man emerge from the aforesaid dawn and pour his brightness over the aforementioned darkness; it repulsed him; he turned blood-red and pallid, but struck back against the darkness with such force that the man who was lying in the darkness became visible and resplendent through this contact, and standing up, he came forth out of the darkness.'[39] Contact with light has power to expose, to heal and to bring forth the human being 'resplendent'. In a follow-on vision Hildegard sees the same light-filled man she had seen previously. He denudes the children made black from sin and clothes them in new garments of light: 'And behold, that serene light, with the figure of a man in it, blazing with a glowing fire, which I had seen in my previous vision [II, 2.13–21], again appeared to me, and stripped the black skin off each of them and threw it away; and it clothed each of them in a pure white garment and opened to them the serene light.'[40]

Hildegard's brilliant vision of a statuesque woman is an allegory of the world made beautiful in the image and vision of God, but whose tattered dress betrays the spoiling and soiling of sin:

> Her face shone with great brightness, and with her eyes she looked into heaven. She was clothed in a garment of dazzling white silk, over which was a cloak set with precious stones – with emeralds, sapphires, and pearls – and on her feet were shoes of onyx. But her face was smudged with dirt, and her dress was torn on the right side. Moreover, her cloak had lost its exquisite beauty, and the tops of her shoes were soiled.[41]

In Hildegard the story of salvation is reiterated in diverse ways. Within the allegorical 'Homilies on the Nativity' there are traces of the notion of deification. The following extract shows that the birth of Christ brings the gift of rationality to elevate humanity into the light of God's precepts, and to uplift human thoughts into the ways of God. Joseph has to go up in an ascent to Bethlehem, to the site of the incarnation, which figuratively speaking, is the seat of rationality. Joseph represents unenlightened human beings; Mary, by virtue of her conception of the Word, is the bearer of rationality. The birth of Jesus Christ is the birth of rationality, that is, the Word of God, the rationality imparted to Joseph for enlightenment:

> And Joseph from Galilee, from the city of Nazareth . . . went up into Judea to the city of David . . . which is called Bethlehem, which had rationality . . . with his espoused wife, Mary, that is, with the rationality given to him . . . And it came to pass when they were there, that is, when the human being had discretion in rationality, the days were fulfilled that she should be delivered, when with hearing he received the precept of God.[42]

Ascension into rationality is only one side of the coin in the complex problem of human change. The exchange of the old nature for the new is the work, as it were, of the counsellor of the exchequer, the Holy Spirit. In a compelling image Hildegard describes the entire human nature pervaded by the Spirit: 'As cheap food is changed by the taste of spices into better tasting food, losing its poor taste, so by the fire of the Holy Spirit the human's cheap nature is changed into a better nature than their conception implies. And thus human beings become different in nature, because what is heavenly conquers and overcomes what is earthly'.[43] The formation of the *imago Dei* by the Holy Spirit is codified everywhere in the corpus in extensive figures of speech which draw on the four elements of earth, air, water and fire. For example, spiritual growth in the gospel parable of the sower (Mark 4:3–9,13–20) is narrated by means of the combined elements of earth and water: 'the seed of your heart will be multiplied and placed in a clear light because you have sown on good soil that which has been watered with the grace of the Holy Spirit'.[44] Water as an agent of cleansing is a common image for the sanctifying Spirit in Hildegard: 'The living fountain is the Spirit of God . . . all his works have living life through that fountain, as the shadow of all things appears in water'.[45] Hence all the works of creation find their source in the living well of the Spirit. The creature is satisfied with abundance through the Spirit's spring of life: 'Turn your mind back again to wholesome things, and look into the fountain of dancing water' [John 4:14].[46] The scriptural allusions to the properties of water as purifier, cleanser, thirst-quencher and life-giver show that all these are gifts of the Spirit for human beings (John 4:10; 7:37–39; Acts 1:4; 2:38; 10:45; Rev. 22:17). The agent of the baptism of fire (Matt. 3:11; Luke 3:16) is the Spirit: 'by the fiery heat understand the Holy Spirit, who burns ardently in the minds of the faithful'.[47] The combined elements of water and fire illustrate the Spirit's task as sanctifier of the church: 'This means that the multitude that is in the Catholic faith are given many things by the fire of the Holy Spirit, who sprinkles their minds'.[48] At one point Hildegard's imagery of breath extends beyond the idea of exhalation, used in antiquity in the literal sense, and by her contemporary, the medical writer Maurus of Salerno (1130–1214), of human breathing. The elements of fire and breath are unified in the Spirit's operation so that the 'fire of [God's] gifts' (*'ignis donorum'*) becomes the 'breath' (*'exspiratio'*) of God's gifts.[49]

The narration of the drama of salvation is told by Hildegard not only in song and vision, but also in a morality play, 'Play of the Virtues', a dramatic presentation of a fierce battle between the virtues and the vices for possession of the human soul. If we are able to pass beyond the peculiarities of the image, we will find Christ personified as a dynamic figure of war, this time as the champion who comes to the rescue through his death on the cross. The

'Finale' is Hildegard's way of representing the agony of the crucifixion and the words from the cross. Poignantly, the champion
speaks to his Father of his utter fatigue, the physical breakdown of
his body, the collapse of his limbs derided in public spectacle. In
distress he offers to his Father his wounded body, the sacrifice
decided upon at the beginning of the dryness, the rebellion of earth.
His wounds are on show like beautiful jewels for his Father to see:

> And the champion saw this and said . . .
> 'In my body I am suffering exhaustion,
> even my little ones faint.
> Now remember that the fullness which was made in the beginning
> need not have grown dry,
> and that then you resolved
> that your eye would never fail
> until you saw my body full of jewels.
> For it wearies me that all my limbs are exposed to mockery:
> Father, behold, I am showing you my wounds'.[50]

In the closing lines of the 'Finale', the playwright compresses the
work of the cross as an historic event, into a timeless never-
ending coming again of Christ, and his claim on the soul. Hildegard reaches out to the audience in a striking appeal, reminiscent
of a twenty-first-century evangelistic, gospel 'altar call', an invitation to surrender, to clasp the hand of the Father:

> So now, all you people,
> bend your knees to the Father,
> that he may reach you his hand.[51]

If the hand of the Father represents the Son then we have come
full circle to Irenaeus and the significance of the metaphor of the
two hands of God. In Hildegard's vision in *Scivias*, the champion
returns at the closing of the age in dazzling glory with his beautiful wounds clearly visible: 'And suddenly from the East a great
brilliance shone forth; and there, in a cloud, I saw the Son of Man,
with the same appearance he had had in the world and with his
wounds still open, coming with the angelic choirs. He sat upon a
throne of flame, glowing but not burning'.[52]

Trinity in community

The 'Hymn to Saint Ursula' in *Symphonia* draws together a novel coalition of prophetic ideas about suffering. There is the martyrdom of Ursula and the one thousand virgins, which shouts from the earth like the blood of Abel (Gen. 4:10, cf. Heb. 12:24). Then there is the reference to the visitation of the three angelic beings to Abraham at the oaks of Mamre (Gen. 18:1–15), which the church fathers saw as a foreshadowing of the later revelation of the Trinity. The prophet exclaims, 'This blood is touching us!' and we are uncertain if this refers to the community of the church, which cannot remain immune to the tragedy, or to the Trinity, which must open its arms to embrace human pain:

> When the voice of Ursula's blood
> and the blood of her innocent
> flock cried like Abel's
> before the throne of God,
> an ancient prophet came forth -
> he who saw the truth
> of the Trinity by the oaks
> of Mamre – and he said:
> This blood is touching us![53]

The unlimited hermeneutical horizon in the text is an incredible vista for prophecy. It points to a bond of suffering within the community of the Trinity, between the Trinity and the human community and between human communities past and present. It leads directly to the community of the cross in Bonhoeffer, to solidarity between Christ and the world's people, to a stance which appears closer to our theological gaze at the beginning of our century than the medieval close-at-hand heaven in Hildegard. If Hildegard is obtuse and radically out there, then Bonhoeffer is in here, in the centre of everything human, in the heart of the cross and the crucified Jesus.

Dietrich Bonhoeffer: Community of the Cross

> I do not know who this man Jesus Christ is unless I say at the same
> time 'Jesus Christ is God', and I do not know who the God Jesus
> Christ is unless I say at the same time 'Jesus Christ is man'
> (Dietrich Bonhoeffer).[54]

Like Hildegard's tussle with theologians of her day, Bonhoeffer's theological conclusions are very often the result of a dialogical process with philosophers and theologians, in fields similar, or dissimilar, to his own explorations. Unlike Hildegard's reliance on her spiritual *visio*, in Bonhoeffer we have to do with a complicated cognitive process. We may be assisted in our task of making sense of the field and identifying the exact components of his vision, by a convenient analogy of a lens. A lens is a piece of glass, either bringing together or spreading rays of light passing through it, used in optical instruments to form an image. The preceding chapters attempted to trace the progression of Bonhoeffer's theology of the Word from the first period of formation, head to head with the liberal Berlin academy and shoulder to shoulder with the Barthian dialectic, to the middle period of crisis theology, tested to its limits in a radical climate of a nation on the brink of war. German liberalism and crisis theology provided a lens through which Bonhoeffer's thought passed, either clarifying or diffusing his vision.

The concentration in this chapter is upon the person of Jesus Christ and touches upon the theology of the reformer Martin Luther and the philosophy of the atheist Ludwig Feuerbach (1804–72) as a lens through which Bonhoeffer's thought passes to illuminate his own vision. It must be stressed that neither thinker is the only lens for the topic, but as this work is concerned with prophecy, and is not a composite analysis of Bonhoeffer's corpus, it may be considered a small beginning. This particular examination of the person of Jesus is understood through the notions of *theologia crucis* (theology of the cross) and 'Christ existing as church-community'. Data is formulated from first, middle and final periods of the corpus and is used freely throughout the discussion. The chapter is ordered according to two searching interrogatives in Bonhoeffer: 'Who is Jesus Christ?' and 'Where is Jesus Christ?'[55]

Who is Jesus Christ?

Bonhoeffer is deeply preoccupied with the person of Jesus Christ in two places: within the structure of church community in time-space; and within the church sent out into the world to encounter Christ in the other. The accent upon *verus homo* in the God-man binds Christ to true humanity. The church which carries the 'testimony of Jesus' bears the imprint of his cross and suffering. Bonhoeffer disentangles off-putting Christian doctrine relating to the knotty inevitable question to Christian and pagan alike, 'Who do you say that I am?'

Theologia crucis

In our Christian faith we run the risk at times of generalizing or belittling notions which are hard to grasp or do not add up. It is vital that we come to terms with paradoxical opposites. We find a perfect example of this discipline in the construct of *theologia crucis* in Luther, which plays a pivotal role in the development of Bonhoeffer's work on the person of Jesus Christ, the Word of God. Luther's key to the revelation of the Word is its origin, *both* in the hidden God, 'Truly, you are a God who hides himself' (Isa. 45:15), *and* in the revealed God, 'Whoever has seen me has seen the Father' (John 14:9).

In essence, the Word, for Luther, is very God of very God, begotten not made, of one being with the Father, and this revelation is given straight from above, from the Father's heart. In imaginative language Luther sees God pregnant with his Word, i.e. the pre-existent, incarnate co-Creator Christ (Heb. 1:1–3). The Word is in the heart of God, deeply sealed and soon to be revealed. In the *Sermons on the Gospel of St John* he comments on the divine inner dialogue: 'Thus God, too, from all eternity has a Word, a speech, a thought, or a conversation with himself in his divine heart, unknown to angels and men'. The Word is the 'Speech [which] existed from the beginning of the creation of the world, approximately four thousand years before Christ's birth and incarnation; yes, he was in the Father's heart from all eternity'. For Luther the discovery of God is not by means of the pattern of the created order and the nature of moral sense, but through Christ, on whom the Bible and all its contents is centred.

The revelation of God is from above. God is uncovered in the person of his Son, through which the final Word has been spoken.[56]

At one and the same time, however, the revelation is initiated, paradoxically, from below, from the ladder which is Christ. This exposure is indirect and concealed in the crucified Christ, a secret not immediately recognizable and discernible only by faith to the 'friends of the cross'. The crucified Lord discloses God: 'All goods are hidden in and under the cross. Hence they are neither to be sought nor understood except under the cross . . . nothing but "Jesus Christ and him crucified".' The notion of *theologia crucis* condenses the power, wisdom, strength and glory of God into that which is revealed and yet hidden under the cross. Concerning the powerlessness of the godly who suffer oppression Luther remarks, 'There is the fullness of God's power and his outstretched arm. For where man's strength ends, God's strength begins, provided faith is present and waits on him . . . Even so Christ was powerless on the cross; and yet there he performed his mightiest work and conquered sin, death, world, hell, devil, and all evil'.[57]

Downward movement

The relevance of the *theologia crucis* in *Discipleship*, the work completed in Bonhoeffer's middle period, is to the formation of Christ in the believer. The downward movement of the cross is the total identification of the Son with humankind. Two seminal texts support the discussion on the transformation of the disciple: 'Do not be conformed to this world, but be transformed by the renewing of your minds' (Rom. 12:2); 'And all of us, with unveiled faces, seeing the glory of the Lord . . . are being transformed into the same image from one degree of glory to another' (2 Cor. 3:18). Verses from the hymn found in Philippians 2:6–11 emphasize the downward self-emptying movement of Christ into the slave-form and are the basis for Bonhoeffer's analysis of the German word *Gestalt*. Most of us are familiar with the English term 'Gestalt', meaning 'configuration' or 'structure'. The primary meaning of the German word *Gestalt* is 'form', 'shape', 'figure', 'build', 'frame', 'stature', 'air', 'manner', 'aspect', 'fashion', 'kind' or 'character'. The derivative word *Gestaltung* ought to be translated in the first instance as 'configuration', based on the meaning of the verb 'to form', thus *Form* or *Kontur*, translated as 'figuration'.[58]

In *Discipleship* the divine image, *Gestalt*, which had remained with God through eternity, assumes the form of the fallen, rotten human being. God sends the Son in the likeness of corrupt flesh (Rom. 8:2f.). The 'miracle' of the incarnation is Christ configured in pain, inner conflict and death, in the exchange of the divine for the human nature. The good news, in the inability of human beings to conform to the divine pattern, is that it is all up to God: 'God must conform to the human image since we are no longer able to conform to the image of God'. God has drawn near, not in a new idea or a new religion, but in human form: 'In Jesus Christ, God's own image has come into our midst in the form of our lost human life, in the likeness of sinful flesh'. In the exposition of *Gestalt* Bonhoeffer emphasizes the earthly humiliation and abandonment; the wounds of the cross are the reminder of rejection. These same 'marks' and 'wounds' have now become 'signs of grace on the body of the risen and transfigured Christ'.[59] The underlying references to the Suffering Servant of Isaiah in Bonhoeffer mark these passages (Isa. 52:13 – 53:12).

Upward movement

For Bonhoeffer the upward movement of the cross lies in its power to draw humanity into the image of God. Grace is extended, not for the emulation of a pattern of humility, but for participation in the suffering of Christ. In *Discipleship*, suffering with Christ precedes glorification with Christ: 'Whoever seeks to bear the transfigured image of Jesus must first have borne the image of the crucified one, defiled in the world'. The goal is the Christ-form of incarnation, crucifixion and resurrection: 'Our goal is to be shaped into the entire *form* ['Gestalt'] of the *incarnate*, the *crucified*, and the *risen one*'. Conformation to Christ crucified occurs through the form of death: 'The form of Christ on earth is the *form of the death* of the crucified one'. Identifying with Christ in baptism is 'becoming like him in his death' (Phil. 3:10). 'Friends of the cross' are glorified with Christ: 'Those who remain in community with the incarnate and crucified one and in whom he gained his form will also become like the *glorified and risen one*'. The community of the cross shares the image of Christ: 'It is indeed the holy Trinity who dwells within Christians, who permeates them and changes them into the very image of the triune God . . . The church bears the incarnate, crucified, and risen form of Jesus Christ . . . Within the body of Christ we have become "like Christ"'.[60]

Outward movement

In *Discipleship* the Word goes out to form a visible community and that is where Jesus Christ is found: 'The body of the exalted Lord is likewise a visible body, taking the form of the church-community'. The body becomes visible when the Word 'seeks out community in order to accept it'.[61] In *Ethics* Bonhoeffer argues against the right of the church to define itself independently of the *Gestalt* of Jesus Christ. The outward movement of divine formation is double-edged: Christ takes form in the church and universally in the world. The new worldly humanity is drawn into the church and is formed by the image of Christ. Thus 'the real human being receives the form of Christ', crucified and risen.[62]

Bonhoeffer is unable to divorce the outward movement of Christ-formation from the ethical demand. The *Gestalt* of Jesus is hidden under the cross and stakes out space visibly in church and world. The concept of *theologia crucis* is distilled into a deeply personal and costly discipleship, 'Only he who believes is obedient and only he who is obedient believes'. The pithy statement represents Bonhoeffer's interrogation of a forensic and clinical adherence to the doctrine of justification by faith. The Lutheran declaration of the 'righteousness of God' (Rom. 1:17) is 'the chief article of the entire Christian doctrine,' without which no poor conscience can have any abiding comfort or rightly understand the riches of the grace of Christ. A pietistic introspective interpretation of the doctrine, and its use by the German academy, was a calculated barricade against political engagement with Reich ideology. From his prison cell Bonhoeffer argues that the doctrine of justification by faith is never an escape from political reality into pietism: 'Aren't righteousness and the Kingdom of God on earth the focus of everything, and isn't it true that Rom. 3:24ff. is not an individualistic doctrine of salvation, but the culmination of the view that God alone is righteous?'[63] Thus Bonhoeffer challenges our present-day malaise of absorption with personal salvation and the emptying of the cross of its power to shake kingdoms and to establish the kingdom of heaven here on earth.

Stellvertretung

Bonhoeffer's move away from an over-spiritualized emphasis on the doctrine of justification by faith is interwoven with the very fabric of his theological programme. The structure of reality is the *Gestalt* of Jesus Christ crucified, risen and glorified. Therefore, Bonhoeffer seeks to give new meaning to the doctrine by portraying Jesus Christ not only as Saviour, but as our representative. The idea is not new to our study, as we came across it in the analysis of Christ in the cursing psalms. The notion of *Stellvertretung* is associated with the words 'vicarious', 'representative', or 'one who steps into our place', and 'participation'. In a nutshell the concept is that Jesus Christ is 'the very embodiment of the person who lives responsibly . . . His entire life, action, and suffering is vicarious representative action'. From the example of Christ it follows that 'the structure of responsible life is determined in a twofold manner, namely, by life's bond to human beings and to God, and by the freedom of one's own life'. These texts in *Ethics* are the culmination of Bonhoeffer's thought on the topic to that point.[64]

A quick glance at the earlier works reveals the complexity of a double action: the vicarious redemption of Christ and the surrender, therefore, in vicarious action of human beings one to another. In *Sanctorum Communio* the problem and principle of vicarious action is set out in this dual fashion, as Christ's action, and as the structure of responsible life. By the triumph of a criminal's cross, a pure vicarious deed, Christ took the blame for sin.[65] In *Discipleship* vicarious suffering has already been accomplished by Christ stepping into our place. The locus for vicarious action is the community, which represents the world before God, or a small group, which represents the whole community.[66] In *Sanctorum Communio* and *Discipleship* the benefit of Christ's vicarious action is accrued to us and our response is to copy that pattern.[67] In *Life Together* the mark of vicarious action is an attitude of bearing with one another. A Christian stands in Christ's place as the sign of God's truth and grace.[68] In *Ethics* the life of responsibility takes it measure from Christ's own human life lived vicariously as our representative.

Christ is the real responsible human being because of whom we can live responsibly towards other human beings.[69]

Community of the cross
Our spiritual difficulty is often the management of head and heart. This is not the case in Bonhoeffer. As a theologian he refuses a theory of cognition: head at the expense of heart is never his intention. As an academic his pursuit is relational. He wants to enjoy relationship with God and friendship with neighbour. On Trinity Sunday in 1932 he states: 'Christ did not come into the world that we might understand him, but that we should cling to him'. In an Advent sermon in 1928 he expounds on Matthew 25:31–46 on the coming again of Christ (Rev. 3:20) in 'the form of a beggar, in the form of a ruined human being in torn clothing . . . in every person that you meet. Christ walks on the earth as your neighbour as long as there are people'. His devotion and witness, stated as clinging to Christ and meeting Christ incognito in your neighbour, is captured in a meditation by the well-known spiritual icon, Mother Teresa of Calcutta (1910–97): 'once more Christ came in distressing disguise – in the hungry man, in the lonely man, in the homeless child, seeking shelter'.[70]

Bonhoeffer's reflection on the theology of the cross in the early and middle period discloses God concealed in the weakness of the cross and contracted into the 'other' person in church. The church tells the story of the cross as a visible presence in the world. The writings in the final Tegel period push the theology of the cross into a church of the cross, and are a summons to Christians not to flee this world but to journey towards it in sacrificial love. In the world they will find Jesus, truly man, incognito in outcast and sinner. To be simultaneously at one with Christ, and with the world, is the realization that 'by living completely in this world', at once 'we throw ourselves completely into the arms of God, taking seriously not our own sufferings, but those of God in the world – watching with Christ in Gethsemane'. To participate in Christ is to share his sufferings in this world and not to escape into a world to come: 'like Christ himself . . . [the Christian] must drink the earthly cup to the dregs, and only in his doing so is the crucified and risen Lord with him'. In a singular description of abandonment, 'God lets himself be pushed out of the world on to the cross', Bonhoeffer depicts the task of the Christian as keeping watch with Christ and sharing in God's impotence against every possibility of escape into numbness.[71]

The conviction that Christians should stand on the outskirts of society with the world's despised, in the Man for others, the crucified Jesus, incognito in outcast and reject, is exemplified in the life of Bonhoeffer, the patriot, who died incognito for love of Germany and offers in himself a prophetic testimony to Jesus in his identification with Christ as *verus homo*. Bonhoeffer's life is vividly depicted as the 'testimony of Jesus' in the epitaph on the wall of a village church in Flossenbürg: 'Dietrich Bonhoeffer – Witness for Jesus Christ among His Brothers'.[72]

Where is Jesus Christ?

In Chapter 1 we discovered Bonhoeffer's frustration with a faraway God in the early period and his desire to bring God nearer to us. In order to accomplish this successfully he draws heavily upon the insights of philosophy, thus going outside strictly scriptural boundaries, which may be unacceptable or foreign to some. Bonhoeffer works in an opposite manner to Hildegard, who avoids the employment of the philosophical thought of her day. In *Act and Being* Bonhoeffer reworks the abstract philosophical notion of *Dasein* (existence), as Being-enclosed and self-enclosed finitude, into concrete Christian terms. True human existence is 'being-in-Christ'; genuine humanity and self-understanding are actualized in the contract between Christ and the human person. The very early work, *Sanctorum Communio*, Bonhoeffer's qualification for licentiate in 1927, was a sociological analysis of the church. In it he attempts to bring God nearer in a self-binding of God to the historical revelation in Jesus Christ. He adapts the phrase of the philosopher G.W.F. Hegel (1770–1831), 'God existing as community', into 'Christ existing as church-community'. By exchanging a theory of *Geist* (the presence of God in the world as Absolute Spirit or objective will in community) for Christ as 'collective person', he adds an incarnational aspect and identifies Christ with the church.[73] This was the thought behind *Sanctorum Communio*: 'Where the body of Christ is, there Christ truly is. Christ is in the church-community, as the church-community is in Christ.'[74]

Bonhoeffer demonstrates that God inhabits the world, not as Absolute Spirit, but as 'Christ existing as church-community'. Being-in-Christ, therefore, is the human being drawn into the church and drawn at the same time into true humanity. This scheme overcomes abstract speculative philosophy and positions the estranged 'I' in the middle of a holy society which is dominated by God's presence and not by his absence.

Christ existing as church-community
In his dogged persistence to entwine God and humanity in social categories, Bonhoeffer strikes upon his own concept, borrowed from philosophical categories, of 'Christ existing as church-community'. The community of the holy (*sanctorum communio*) has its sole dependency upon the supernatural revelation of the Word, which is not sheer talk about Christ, but is the person of Christ himself with his people. This view of ultimate reality is therefore a concrete vision of the reality which is Jesus Christ: 'The proclaimed Word is the Incarnate Christ himself . . . The preached Christ is the historical Christ and the present Christ . . . He is the entrance to the historical Jesus. Therefore, the proclaimed Word is not a medium of expression for something else, something which lies behind it, but it is the Christ himself walking through his community as the Word.'[75] In this positive vision of human community the note struck most meaningfully is that solitariness, isolation and alienation are overcome in a body of people among whom Christ lives. The construct exhibits an ecclesiological optimism which resonates with that of the church fathers, who saw the church not as an institution, but as a way of being, and membership of the church, therefore, as the assuming of God's manner of being.[76] The concept that true humanity is being-in-Christ has the potency of the universal, and offers a vista to be recovered for prophetic perspective. In our contemporary age a prophetic vision of Jesus Christ in the world offers an antidote for alienation which fosters despair, lack of personal vision, cynicism or pessimism. A prophetic interpretation of being-in-Christ, for a twenty-first-century global village, means that a Christian can never exist without the consciousness of the other as a fellow traveller, in a network of relationships with its obligations and responsibilities.

Man for others

As we continue to survey Bonhoeffer's dialogue with the philosophers, we experience not only his dallying with their theories, but also his critique. De Lubac believes that absolute humanism eliminates God in order to regain and repossess human greatness and liberty from the obstacle withholding it, i.e. God. This philosophy is epitomized in the arch-opponent to Christianity, Ludwig Feuerbach, whose schema destroys the *imago Dei*.[77] His plausible claim, that 'only what is real is true', cleverly removes the image of God in the human being, as 'any object can become a god, or what amounts to the same thing, an object of religious worship'.[78] Feuerbach's idea of what is genuine, or the really real, is the replacement of 'the love of God by the love of man as the only true religion'.[79] For Feuerbach, God is an invention of the human mind. In the Preface to the second edition of his work *The Essence of Christianity*, he argues that religion has made man into God, man with a human form, human feelings and thoughts. This man has been turned into an object of veneration; thus the idea of a Son of God is simply absurd. He is quite aware that his work is negative, controversial and destructive, but he wants to oppose religion forcefully as 'the dream of the human mind'.[80]

Bonhoeffer undertakes an extremely convincing counter-argument to that of his rival. He recognizes that Feuerbach's grilling of Christianity is directed at the truth of the church's propositions and their relevance to real life.[81] In *Act and Being* he attempts to break through Feuerbach's abstraction, in the real-ity of a personal God in relationship: 'There is no God who "is there"; God "is" in the relation of persons, and being is God's being person'.[82] The development of God's concreteness in the poem 'Night Voices in Tegel', written from prison in 1944, is a striking reclamation of the image of God in human 'brotherliness':

> Brother, till the night be past
> Pray for me!
> Brother, when the sun turns pale for me,
> Then live for me.[83]

The second stanza of the prison poem 'Christians and Pagans' constitutes Bonhoeffer's tender retort to a vampire God. In place of a hungry tyrant is a defenceless, weak God eaten by the monster of human sin:

> People turn to God in God's own need,
> and find God poor, degraded, without roof or bread,
> see God devoured by sin, weakness, and death.
> Christians stand with God to share God's pain.[84]

Bonhoeffer's 'Notes' at the beginning of the Tegel incarceration mourn the loss of the people of God: 'Separation from people/ from work/from the past/from the future/from marriage/from God'. Then 'Dissatisfaction/Tension/Impatience/Longing/ Boredom/sick – profoundly alone/Indifference', then 'Suicide, not because of consciousness of guilt but because basically I am already dead, draw a line/Overcoming in *prayer*'.[85]

Verus homo

Bonhoeffer's theological task is to answer the question, 'How is faith true and real?' by pointing to the person of Jesus Christ, and asking, 'Who is Christ for us today?' The domination of Jesus as *verus homo* clearly indicates that in Bonhoeffer's theological vision 'the testimony of Jesus is the Spirit of prophecy'. The advent of the person of Jesus, as 'the beyond in the midst of life', brings the sanctification of the sinful human being within reach. The problem, however, with the privileging of *verus homo* is the danger that the contraction of the godhead into human form produces a mere 'suffering man for others', condenses the infinite completely into the finite, and blurs the distinction between God and the church. If Jesus is understood only as the man *with* us, shrunk into the world in concrete 'this-worldliness', does it not emasculate him as *verus Deus*, God *with* us, rescuer *from* adversity and for a greater life?

Verus Deus/Verus Homo

If our target is the 'testimony of Jesus' then how do Hildegard and Bonhoeffer reflect this, we may ask? Hildegard's *visio* is one woman's enraptured encounter with the persons in Trinity.

Bonhoeffer's scheme leads to encounter in human community. Both are valid. Both are true. If transfiguring life in Hildegard is found in the supernatural light of God, then transformation in Bonhoeffer cannot take place without costly discipleship in the darkness of pain and suffering. In Bonhoeffer the 'hand' of Jesus is magnified. In Hildegard the 'hand' of Christ is one of two, the 'hand' of the Spirit plainly operative in her Trinitarian *visio*. Bonhoeffer's weakness in elucidating clearly the *how* of discipleship, as it concerns the role of the Holy Spirit in the following of the Crucified, is, as it were, taken up in Hildegard to complement the Trinitarian story. We have been shown in numerous passages on the elemental Spirit that in Hildegard the present operation of the Spirit in the life of the believer is of the utmost value.

Attention to the two paths of medieval mysticism and Jesus-focused twentieth-century humanitarianism has shown that their vapour trails overlap at certain points and are not incompatible: desire for God and love of neighbour; the beams of the cross are vertical and horizontal, arms wide open. The primary Christological traditions we have ascertained in Hildegard and Bonhoeffer may now be combined: encounters with the heavenly Trinity and the Man for others, the conformation of the disciple into the image of God with the help of the Holy Spirit, the Helper. The combining power of these impulses in Bonhoeffer and Hildegard will ensure that Christian deeds of charity are not neglected and that the body of believers together becomes a shining light in a dark world. What we seek at the outset of the third millennium is not simply a humanitarian sentiment of good works and deeds, or an other-worldly cosmic world-denying force, but a personal relationship with the persons of the Trinity, God the Father, Son and Holy Spirit, within the community of faith, which is itself in constant process of bending outwards into a needy world, as a move of love to embrace the alienated. Is not the development of communities of love, touched by the supernatural graces of God, in intimate communion with the Trinitarian persons and intricately involved with the wider world, a longing implanted supernaturally by the Father of lights? Will these communities of healing, divine sparks to offset the darkness, not be prophetic witnesses and so fulfil the 'testimony of Jesus' as 'the Spirit of prophecy'?

4.

VISIONARY DREAMERS

> Now the Spirit shows forth the Word, and therefore the prophets
> announced the Son of God; and the Word utters the Spirit, and
> therefore is himself the announcer of the Prophets (Irenaeus).[1]

In the previous chapter we discussed the person of Jesus Christ,
the Word, and the first of the two 'hands' of God. We scrutinized
the phrase, 'the testimony of Jesus is the Spirit of prophecy', in
order to come to grips with the focus on Jesus in the theologies of
our two prophets. We saw that the communities of the human
and the divine in Hildegard and Bonhoeffer each are a group
with a spotlight beamed on the Second Person of the Trinity. We
noted their points of departure as products of their distinctive
spiritual climates and the air they breathed: Jesus viewed from
above or from below. In this chapter our concern is the question:
How is the Spirit promoted in Hildegard and Bonhoeffer to the
position of a herald who announces the testimony of Jesus?
Although we have already touched on the function of the Spirit,
we will examine more intently the Spirit as the other 'hand' of
God, the one behind it all, directing the operation not simply as a
sheer impersonal force, nor an objective dynamism, nor an amor-
phous essence or vaporous air, nor even another Jesus, but as a
blessed and beloved, uniquely himself, Third *Person* in the Holy
Trinity.

Spiritual Cataracts

The questions surrounding the authenticity and reliability of visions and dreams must be addressed with reference to their mainspring. What is the fountainhead or originating source for a theological or spiritually prophetic vision? What nativity induces such a child? In the biblical tradition there is no end to stories of true prophets who are caught up lightly in the slipstream of the Spirit or driven in a torrential deluge of a spiritual cataract where they are catapulted and lifted into mysteries unknown. Our problem today is dim vision, half-sightedness and spiritual cataracts over the eyes of the church:

> he has closed your eyes, you prophets,
>   and covered your heads, you seers.

> The vision of all this has become for you like the words of a sealed document. If it is given to those who can read with the command 'Read this', they say, 'We cannot, for it is sealed.' And if it is given to those who cannot read, saying, 'Read this', they say, 'We cannot read' (Isa. 29:10b–12).

A clue to the visionary blindness or partial sightedness of the church today lies in our antipathy to the supernatural. We need to chart a path back to its complete recovery in order to actualize the breadth and depth of the work of the Holy Spirit. De Lubac, one of the exemplars of the movement of *ressourcement*, holds a key. He may appear passé, an outdated regressive overtaken by others more noteworthy, but his work bears rereading to those seeking ongoing theological renewal. John Milbank, a leading thinker in the theological circle of Radical Orthodoxy, suggests that de Lubac is arguably one of the greatest theologians of the twentieth century. He posits that de Lubac offers a major cultural revision: our 'desire' for God will disclose reality to us and not our own 'capacity' or 'power', which is the primitive pagan philosophical assumption.[2] In *Catholicism* de Lubac writes: 'The vision of God is a free gift, and yet the desire of it is at the very root of every soul'.[3] The fundamental truth for which he contends in *The Mystery of the Supernatural* is that God never ceases to draw us towards himself because he has made us for himself. The secular agenda separates us from God in the name of Christian progress and the entry into adulthood, exiling God from society, culture and personal relationship. Secularism downplays the supernatural as no more than a 'super-nature' so that the supernatural is no longer another order, 'something unprecedented, overwhelming and transfiguring'. De Lubac is quick to assert the paradox of the vision of God: on the one hand there is a deeply implanted human longing to see God and a natural desire for God; on the other this 'infusion of grace' comes as a divine gift.[4] For de Lubac the temporal is always lifted up into eternity; when Christians, therefore, look only to the natural world for 'signs' of the nature of God, they lose sight of his free gift, the natural world being merely an end in itself.[5]

In this chapter we will look more closely at the Spirit, whose property it is to tear away the blindfolds, to remove the veil to see the future, to lift our sights to the unattainable and impossible, to minister a healing balm to the eyes of the church (Rev. 3:18). With a view to recovering a theology of the operation of the Spirit in the gift of prophecy, we can be certain of a biblical patristic-medieval schema. A search party with a dragnet cannot fail to pull up treasures from these depths.

The Person of the Holy Spirit

The text 2 Peter 1:20–21 succinctly clarifies the genesis of prophetic utterance: 'First of all you must understand this, that no prophecy of Scripture is a matter of one's own interpretation, because no prophecy ever came by human will, but men and women moved by the Holy Spirit spoke from God.' Clearly the power behind the vision or dream is not the enthusiasm of the visionary or dreamer but the person of the Spirit. There are two ways to exegete this passage. The first exegesis binds the phrase, 'all prophecy of Scripture' ('*pasa prophēteia graphēs*'), very firmly to prophecies as they have already appeared in the Old Testament. Those who wrote or spoke them did so, not according to their own explanation ('*idias epilyseōs*'), but according to words given straight from God. The word 'interpretation' ('*epilysis*') is virtually equivalent then to 'inspiration'. The problem with this reading is not the matter of inspired text. We are generally agreed that the ancient prophets acted and spoke inspirationally, with a word for Israel which has application for the church today. The difficulty with the reading is that it imprisons prophecy right there in the Old Testament, and the free gift of prophecy (Rom. 12:6; 1 Cor. 12:10,28; 14:1,3,4,22,24,29,31–32,37; Eph. 4:11), loosened and unbound for the present day, is not an option.[6]

The second analysis is the majority view that the verse has to do with a prophetic interpretation intended by the Spirit for the current situation. The word '*epilysis*' means a right interpretation not influenced by personal agendas or flights of fancy. The biblical distinction between false and true prophecy is upheld, that the former is generated from the mind of the prophet (Jer. 23:16; Ezek. 13:3), whereas the latter is dependent on the mind of the prophet under the influence of the Spirit (Mark 12:36; Acts 3:21; 2 Tim. 3:16; Heb. 1:1). This is brought out plainly in verse 21 through the use of the verb *pherein* ('to impel') in the phrase, 'men and women impelled ['*pheromenoi*'] by the Holy Spirit spoke from God', used in the same sense as in Acts 27:15,17 of a ship driven by wind, 'we . . . were driven' ('*epherometha*'), and the ship caught by wind, 'they . . . were driven' ('*epheronto*').[7]

In Chapter 3 we considered Trinity as community. We passed briefly over Augustine's Trinitarian statement in his treatise *The Trinity*: 'But I do assert with absolute confidence that the Father, the Son, and the Holy Spirit, being of one and the same substance, God the Creator, the omnipotent Trinity, work together inseparably'. We looked at the notion of 'inseparability', the affirmation of essence or substance, the divine persons in their personhood. But Augustine also wants to stress the uniqueness of each person and their relation to one another as community: '[L]et us believe that the Father, the Son, and the Holy Spirit are one God, the Creator, and the ruler of the whole creature; that the Father is not the Son, nor is the Holy Spirit the Father or the Son, but that there is a trinity of inter-related persons, and the unity of an equal substance'. Thus he defends the person of the Spirit by reminding his readers that the Spirit has equal status to Father and Son: 'He is God Himself and not a creature, but if He is not a creature He is not only God (for even men are called gods), but He is also the true God'.[8]

Much emphasis in pneumatology is always given to the Augustinian 'bond of love', that is, the Spirit as the source of harmony in the godhead or the go-between God, but often at the expense of the Spirit as person. The Spirit is indeed the concord between Father and Son, wrapping the world in a divine embrace, moving us into fellowship with one another and the creation. But this 'agreement' is a holy alliance between friends; and the Spirit is not only a divine energy or impulse but a third *person* who completes the mutual love between the other two persons. Augustine writes: 'If by that Holy Spirit . . . a person in the Trinity is understood, that is to say, if by the Holy Spirit is meant the person to whom it properly belongs, then it denotes a relation. For He is referred to both the Father and the Son, because the Holy Spirit is the Spirit of the Father and the Son'. Moreover, Augustine states, the Spirit is not made apparent in the relational name, 'Spirit of the Father and the Son', but is revealed when he is called the 'gift of God'. The word 'gift' signifies the relationship both as Father and Spirit, and Son and Spirit. He is the gift of both.[9] Jesus Christ offers the 'gift of God' when he tells the woman of Samaria to ask for a drink of 'living water' (John 4:10). Peter chides the magician for thinking that money could buy 'God's gift' (Acts 8:20).

The idea of the 'inseparability' of the persons in the Trinity in the patristic church is neatly defined in a catchphrase in the medieval church: 'What One does All do'; similarly 'Alfred is England'. All three persons operated at the creation; the whole deity became incarnate through the Son; the Trinity was involved at Pentecost in the descent of the Spirit and the mission of God. The teaching of the early church is that the Spirit in particular enables human participation in the divine life. Thus the Spirit is 'fountain of wisdom' for inspiration, teacher of souls creating lovers of God, dispenser of huge amounts of justifying saving grace, finger of God fighting for human beings, witness to Christ within the soul. The Holy Spirit is present everywhere personally (*personaliter*), and the outworking of his personal life is shown most fully in the saving actions in the soul. The medieval church consistently upheld the doctrine of Trinitarian 'inseparability', the one is the many, and the Spirit as the medium through whom union with God is attainable.[10]

Hildegard of Bingen: Supernatural *Visio*

> I was in the Spirit on the Lord's day, and I heard behind me a loud voice like a trumpet saying, 'Write in a book what you see' (The Revelation to John 1:10–11a).

An extract from the 'Life of Hildegard' shows how both Word and Spirit operate together to inspire the seer. In a rather curious image the grace of the Spirit is envisaged as the hand of Christ: '[he] *sent forth his hand* (Song 5:4) that is, the operation and inspiration of the Holy Spirit, *through the key-hole*, that is, through his secret grace, and *her entrails*, by which is meant her mind, *trembled at his touch*, that is, at the infusion of his grace'.[11]

The prophetic Spirit

Rupert of Deutz prioritizes the gift of prophecy in his list of the three operations of the Holy Spirit: 'second, in order that human creation might be adorned with spiritual gifts, among which the greatest is that which he has spoken through the prophets'.[12] In the following texts from Hildegard the gifts given by the prophetic Spirit bequeath boldness and soundness of mind (2 Tim. 1:6–7).

The visionary trilogy

In *Divine Works* the Spirit operates as a Principle of Life or energizing Life, through which participation in God is made possible. Hildegard enunciates this energizing Life Principle: 'I awaken the universe with a breath of air as with the invisible life that contains everything'.[13] The Spirit is the regenerating breath which issues from the eternal fire encircling the firmament: 'And so there emerges from this might a breath and the mysterious gifts of the Holy Spirit touch us human beings, who have begun to become dull as a result of boredom. As a result, we shall awaken from our dullness and arise vigorously toward justice'.[14] This imagery resonates with the vision of the valley of the dry bones (Ezek. 37:1–10) and patterns of creation and renewal (Ps. 104:30). The Spirit fires the early apostles with miracles, in the same miraculous way that the skies were first set in place: 'As the firmament accomplishes all its offices with fire, so the apostles, in their miracles, were fired by the Pentecostal Spirit'.[15] In a striking image in *Rewards of Life* Hildegard paints the birth of the church's mission as the Lion of Judah roaring into the wind, expelling the breath of the Spirit to fill the disciples to bursting point to preach: 'For he cried aloud with the inspiration of the Holy Spirit and touched his disciples with the Holy Spirit as he commanded them to preach.'[16] The prophetic Spirit is the 'finger' of God who anoints Scripture with fresh revelation: 'The finger of God had also written on that book the secrets he wished to reveal. This means that the Holy Spirit [poured over] the reason of man as he prophesied'.[17] The implication is that of a wetting or moistening of the mind of the prophet with the living waters of the Spirit. In *Divine Works*, acts of justice become good works of holiness when watered by the Spirit: 'It is justice which, when sprinkled by the dew of the Holy Spirit, ought to germinate good works through holiness'.[18]

In a text from *Rewards of Life* Hildegard lucidly depicts the Holy Spirit as personal and formative in the human longing for a vision of heaven. Those people who align themselves with the Spirit enjoy the virtue called Contempt of the World; those who do not befriend the Spirit and deride heavenly matters will have to pay the penalty: 'For they endure the punishment they have earned since they did not sit with the figure of the Holy Spirit and did not desire the things of heaven'. In comparison Hildegard is one of the virtuous ones who despise the world: 'I, however, sit with the figure of the Holy Spirit'.[19] She will enjoy the rewards bestowed upon a companion of the Spirit and especially that she will prophesy (1 Cor. 14:1).

The letters

We may be startled at the boldness with which Hildegard addresses learned and high-up ecclesiastical dignitaries. However, she leans heavily upon the support of the Holy Spirit for her admonitions to the bishops of the church. In these letters her ally and collaborator is the Spirit, in whose counsel she, too, stands to give direction and warning to prelates in power. To the Shepherds of the church it is the Spirit who provokes a decision from the clergy to rid the area of heretics: 'And the Spirit of God says to you: Look to your city and your district, and cast out those wicked men from your midst'.[20] The severity of Hildegard's warning to Gunther, count of Henneberg and favourite of Frederick I, Barbarossa, is not tempered but heightened by the Holy Spirit: 'The Light of divine inspiration says to you, O man: Do not ignore the admonition of the Holy Spirit through negligence in office'.[21] The letter to Heinrich, archbishop of Mainz, calls upon the voice of the Spirit to issue a prophetic challenge: 'The Spirit of God says earnestly: O shepherds, wail and mourn over the present time, because you do not know what you are doing'.[22]

The songs

We may be surprised that a medieval monastic, not being a flamboyant Pentecostal, has such a liking for the diversity of the Spirit's operations. Five chants in the *Symphonia* invoke Hildegard's muse, the fiery Holy Spirit, all of which are appropriate for use during the season of Pentecost. They illustrate the multitasked diversity of the person of the Spirit who is life-giver, healer, divine love, companion to the virtuous, fighter of temptation and sin, world soul who brings together microcosm and macrocosm in one harmonious universe.[23] There are undercurrents in these verses of the anointing of the Spirit in the messianic community, for example, Isaiah 61:1; Luke 4:18, 11:20 and Acts 10:38. There are times in the translation of these chants when the accent is laid upon the personal and the feminine curative attributes of the Holy Spirit. The Spirit is a healing medic:

> Scrubbing out sins,
> She rubs oil into wounds.
> She is glistening life[24]

The balm of the Spirit is medicinal to all of creation, both soul and body. The text we examined in Chapter 2 shows a circular movement of salvation history, beginning with the champion's jewel-like wounds which become the source of the sanctifying work of the Spirit, who in turn transforms the sores of humanity back into jewels. The work of the Spirit, therefore, continues the saving action of the redeemer in the life of the redeemed.

> So all that live by you
> praise your outpouring
> like a priceless salve upon festering

> sores, upon fractured
> limbs. You convert them
> into priceless gems.[25]

The holiness of the Spirit brings wholeness to the fragmented personality:

> Holy are you, you heal
> The dangerously shattered[26]

In the 'Hymn to the Holy Spirit', heartfelt praise is given to the Third Person of the Trinity, the 'Spirit of fire', whose 'music sets our minds ablaze', so that the rational intellect is made to do homage to the greater God of wisdom:

> Insight invokes you in a cry
> full of sweetness, while reason
> builds you temples as she labours
> at her golden crafts.[27]

In the same sequence (27) the Holy Spirit, with great alacrity, defends those desirous of turning their gaze upon the Tempter, by burning up the passions of the heart:

> When the heart yearns to look
> the Evil One in the eye
> to stare down the jaws of
> iniquity, swiftly
> you burn it in consuming
> fire. Such is your wish.[28]

The Spirit is portrayed as the warrior God combating the evil sword with the same vengeance today as proud Lucifer was overpowered in the very first cosmic battle. These portrayals may allude to the double-edged sword of judgement and discernment in Hebrews 4:12 and Revelation 1:16:

> And when the Evil One brandishes
> his sword against you,

you break it in his own
heart. For so you did
to the first lost angel,
tumbling the tower of his
arrogance to hell.[29]

In 'Antiphon for the Apostles' the Spirit descends in warlike fashion upon the apostles to empower them with strength in their sudden attack on the defence encampment of the 'madmen', probably a reference to demonic forces:

But the Spirit
fell upon you as you stormed
their tents.[30]

Spirit as *personaliter*, therefore, accords with the person of the Spirit in the New Testament as Advocate, Helper, Guide, Baptizer, Spokesperson, Instructor, Encourager, Admonisher, Promise, one who can be grieved, lied against, resisted, obeyed, tested and felt as joy.[31]

Priority of Mary

Those of us who are not of the Catholic tradition may find songs dedicated to Mary most peculiar. The difficulty of the Marian songs in *Symphonia* is not so much their content but their hierarchical position in the cycle. The sequence in manuscript D: 2 songs to the Father, 12 to the Virgin Mary, 5 to the Holy Spirit. Manuscript R corrects this eccentricity: 7 to the Father and the Trinity, 2 to the Spirit, 21 to Mary, followed by 2 to the Spirit. It is generally accepted that of these two manuscripts in which the songs are preserved, D derives directly from Hildegard and is the more authentic.[32]

Hildegard's arrangement of the songs is driven almost entirely by the incarnation and the necessity of the bond between Christ and Mary to accomplish salvation. The gist of Hildegard's conviction may be seen in 'Antiphon for the Virgin' and compared with Anselm in lines from 'Second Prayer to St Mary':

The accused is carried from one to the other
and throws himself between
the good son and the good mother.[33]

Hildegard calls on Mary as rescuer:

> Lend your hand with a shout
> of high auroral praise,
> and lift us frail ones out
> of our bad old ways.[34]

Anselm's prayer invokes both Mother and Son:

> Saviour of each one, tell me whom you will save,
> mother of salvation, tell me for whom you will pray.[35]

Hildegard implores the prayers of the Virgin:

> Mary!
> you plead for us all:
> lift up your voice and carry
> our souls above on the wings of your call.[36]

Hildegard's 'Responsory for the Virgin' lays the emphasis on Mary's role as intercessor in a recurring refrain: 'Pray for us to your child'.[37] Despite their aesthetic and theological appeal, these sentiments overrule the Spirit who knows the mind of God: 'No one comprehends what is truly God's except the Spirit of God' (1 Cor. 2:11). They override the Spirit as interlocutor who knows the will of God and 'intercedes with sighs too deep for words' (Rom. 8:26–27). Little account is taken of the Son who always lives to make intercession on our behalf (Heb. 7:25).

Prophetic dreams

It is highly likely that not a few Christians across the board have no trouble at all with the idea that God speaks to us through dreams, and are already persuaded of their validity. Indeed, those of us of charismatic or Pentecostal persuasion are bombarded with people who dream dreams and have visions. We shall have to get our heads around the view of the twelfth century that a dream is the consequence of human thinking *and* the influence of the demonic or the divine, so that opposites which disagree in the human psyche find resolution in a dream. The human being stands between the divine world of God and pure mind, and the animal kingdom animated only by the life principle. The human being is blessed with reason, vital life *and* spirit, and is capable of receiving both godly and earthly impressions. The dream is a distinguishing mark of being human.[38] In the twelfth century, dreams may be categorized into three types: the higher dream, the dream-poem and the prophetic dream.

The higher dream, different from the human dream described in the above paragraph, is articulated by the word *miraculosus*. This term is an attempt to express a dream which is superlative and of the highest quality or degree. It probably derives from *miraculum*, meaning a wonderful, strange or marvellous thing. The English word 'miraculous', a derivation from the Latin, is that which is supernatural, remarkable or surprising. In a sense, therefore, a dream which is *miraculosus* is literally out of this world. This kind of dream is of a higher order, coming as it does from an ecstatic, meditative state where the one dreaming is caught up beyond the self.

The dream-poem is a genre with defining characteristics. Firstly, there is the narrative of a spiritual journey undertaken in the mind and unconnected to any objective experience. The biblical dreams of Joseph and their influence on Pharaoh, for example, are given as prophetic vision for the economic future of the nation. Secondly, there is the dream of heaven (or hell), which retards the return to the present and suspends the sojourner in temporary limbo. An example of this type is Bede's account of Dryhthelm, who is taken by a guide on a journey through regions unknown to mortals and sees the souls of the dead in hell and heaven.[39]

The dream (*somnium*), as classified by Macrobius (b. early fifth century), is associated with prophetic prediction in that it 'conceals with strange shapes and veils with ambiguity the true meaning of the information being offered, and requires an interpretation for its understanding', so that it 'actually comes true'.[40] The dream depiction of Macrobius is the principal guide for medieval notions of *somnium*. John of Salisbury paints a picture of the prophetic dream which is shrouded in mysterious allegorical figures and images: 'images of events wrapped as it were in a cloak of disguise, and it is with this disguise that the art of interpreting dreams deals', for it 'stretches before the body of truth a curtain, as it were, of allegory'.[44] Having examined a basic premise for medieval dreaming, we must now ask what Hildegard dreams. In what follows we look again at the image of the eagle which, as we have begun to see, is used throughout her corpus, and is expressly significant in the prophet's life.

What the eagle sees

The dreams of Hildegard examined below fall into the categories of *miraculosus* (in the sense of something higher and beyond this world) and *somnium* (in the way of the prophetic). Both are personal dreams which summon Hildegard to awaken from slumber, sickness and self-doubt. Her recurring illnesses are a debilitating factor with power to corrupt her life's work. Her dreams, however, are more powerful and joyously reunite her with her task. They operate like a surgeon to lift her bodily from her bed of sickness and to deposit her directly back into her visionary and prophetic purpose.

Life of Hildegard 2, 9

The first passage alludes to the cosmic battle in Revelation 12:7: 'And war broke out in heaven; Michael and his angels fought against the dragon. The dragon and his angels fought back'. Hildegard's dream recaptures an apocalyptic vision of a battlefield in which the good angels make war against the wicked angels for control of the woman and her offspring, which is an allusion to the nativity of Christ, the Word of God. Unlike the biblical text, however, which is of extraterrestrial proportions, the fight in this battle is for control of the body of Hildegard. Her extreme illness is an attack by the devil and his throng to prevent the birthing of her oracles, the disclosure of the truth of God. Such a fierce battle must be fought to match the importance of the messages she will bring to set people free. The summons to arise finally comes to the dreamer as a great shout, the reference being again to the Revelation, 'and I saw a mighty angel proclaiming with a loud voice' (5:2, cf. 10:1,3). In her dreaming state Hildegard hears one of the throng cry out in the midst of battle:

> 'Come, come, eagle, why are you sleeping in knowledge? Rise from doubt! You will be known. O jewel in brightness, all will see

you, eagle, but the world will grieve, yet will rejoice in eternal life, and so rise as the dawn towards the sun. Rise up, rise up, eat and drink.' And soon the entire battle-array shouted aloud with resounding voice: 'Voice of joy! The messengers were silent: the time of crossing is not yet come. Therefore, get up, girl!' Straightway my body and my frame of mind were returned to their resolute mode of life.[42]

There are many phrases and words in the text which have biblical echoes. In both testaments the figure of the eagle is common as a symbol of prowess, for example, Ezekiel 17:3 or Isaiah 40:31 with its promise of eagles' wings for renewed strength. The Revelation has three usages of the word, each of which could apply to Hildegard. The flying eagle in 4:7 is an allusion in the tradition to the Fourth Gospel, the mystical interpretation akin to the prophetical way in Hildegard, who describes John as 'mild and humble . . . [a man who] drank deeply of divine revelations'.[43] The airborne eagle of judgement in 8:13 and the woman granted the wings of an eagle in 12:14 resonate with Hildegard's vocation and her escape from the devil's clutches. The call is for her to rise up like the sun of righteousness (Mal. 4:2), to bestir herself in the morning like the dawn. She herself is invoked as 'the dawning light', the herald of a new day of hearing God through the messages she will bring. The entire army forcefully enters into the shout of entreaty, again and again, to 'get up', like the daughter of Jairus, for Hildegard's time of crossing over into death has not yet come. The miraculous return of Hildegard's energies of body and soul is the direct result of the potency in the dream which raises her to life to finish the race set before her. Elsewhere in the corpus she compares the eagle's desire for God with the fleeing dawn: 'Just as the eagle in full longing of its heart flies to God, like the dawn'.[44] In such a way does the dream command Hildegard to arise, to flee sickness and to seek God earnestly in the freshness of a new day.

Life of Hildegard 2, 11
'The Life of Hildegard' records one of the many times when Hildegard was beset by a fever. In a dream-like state she sees a number of saints conferring together about the likelihood of her

death. Then suddenly, as though they had all received the same divine permission, they change their minds and chant: 'Then all shouted aloud together, "O happy and most faithful soul, rise up! Rise up just as the eagle, because the sun has led you forth, and you do not know it." And immediately she regained health'.[45] In a similar manner to the first dream examined, the concentration is upon the command, given in this instance by the people of God and not by an angelic host. The word is a divine *fiat*, an order to get up, literally, out of bed. There are scriptural overtones of the imperative voice in Ephesians 5:14:

> Sleeper, awake!
>   Rise from the dead,
> and Christ will shine on you.

The pictorial representation of the eagle is a comfort and a healing strength in Hildegard's plight. The capacity of the eagle to master the skies by soaring on thermals implies that Hildegard, too, will have supernatural vigour to leave sickness behind and to rise with God. The image of the eagle as the most powerful of birds, together with the command in the vocative case, *surge*, 'Arise!', gives to Hildegard not only a remarkable feeling of buoyancy and good health, but the power to be translated from pending death to life.

What the eagle knows

The appearance of an eagle in Hildegard's dreams is a spur to continue the work of seeking the word of the Lord. Throughout her writings she uses this symbol to describe knowledge of God as the most important virtue. In her exposition of Ezekiel 1:10 (cf. Rev. 4:7) she adopts the classical allegorical understanding of the four animals to symbolize the four gospel writers: 'As for the appearance of their faces: the four had the face of a human being, the face of a lion on the right side, the face of an ox on the left side, and the face of an eagle'. In the text there is an underlying stream of consciousness that, of the four, John, the eagle, reigns supreme:

> The face of the eagle prefigures the knowledge of God which gives
> to the human being knowledge and the potential for knowledge,

according to what he desires. It is above the other virtues because in the human being it is an object of terror and it is life to the human being. And this life does not expire but breathes everywhere and sees everywhere, and appears in the human being like stars in the firmament.[46]

The virtue of knowledge of God provokes holy fear which is at once both terrifying and life-giving and as brilliant as stars in the vault of heaven. The revival of knowledge of God during Hildegard's lifetime is exemplified for her by the impulsive, persuasive new spiritualism of the Cistercian reformer Bernard of Clairvaux, who spearheaded the revitalization of monasticism in a visionary breakaway from the smug, static, old Benedictine way. Although he never visited Hildegard's convents, she sings his praises in eagle imagery: 'You move about, but you sustain others. You are assuredly an eagle looking into the sun'.[47] In Hildegard's terminology one who reflects the heavenly light of God and sees him as the angels do is like an eagle: 'Certainly spiritual people, who by every devotion of heart in attentive considering are being marked out by an eagle, frequently contemplate God as angels'.[48]

The power of the supernatural

Hildegard's dreams are prompted by severe spiritual crisis and life-threatening illness, and are resolved by an active influential power beyond her normal consciousness. In the dream she is personified as an eagle not merely to illustrate courage, metaphysically or psychologically. The symbol of the eagle, together with the spoken scriptural command, is the divine supernatural intervention which heals her afflictions and confirms her call. Her dream is paranormal, that is, beyond the scope of objective investigation. In it she actively becomes what she sees. The image of the eagle is a mirror for self-understanding toward a new perceived being, and, having received this revelation of a healed self through the Holy Spirit within the dream, she has the inner power to rise from death to life. What may impress us from this brief summary of the action of the Holy Spirit in Hildegard is the direct application of vision or dream to her life. The 'hand' of the Spirit is strong, vital, and energizing. She is transformed by the operations of the Spirit. She rises up, speaks words of courage and admonishment, and is empowered to follow her call as prophet and teacher. As we study Bonhoeffer's pneumatology, we are forced to see that, apart from the ethical obligation, the Spirit is a fairly dim figure. In his defence we must fall back on the tradition from which he is forged and his entry into the debate over the essentials of faith contested at that time. The taxing question of supernatural manifestation is not his remit. He leans towards Christ at all costs.

Dietrich Bonhoeffer: Creative Speculation

> Where there is no prophecy, the people cast off restraint (Prov. 29:18).

In light of Bonhoeffer's programme to concretize and make Christ present in every aspect of life, the gift of the Holy Spirit would seem to be an integral part of the plan, the operations of the Spirit a necessity to make real the finished work of Christ in the community on earth, as we have observed in Hildegard. Certainly, in the young Bonhoeffer there is a theological record of the role of the Holy Spirit in Lutheran theology. Given the depth of Bonhoeffer's programme, it may surprise us that, although the link between Word and Spirit is an accepted theoretical belief, the application of this is not fleshed out in a pragmatic way in the rest of the corpus. Of the Spirit as the gift given by Christ, or of his gifts or *charismata* for the strengthening of the church, there is no sign (Luke 11:13; John 4:10; 7:39; Acts 2:38; Rom. 12:3–8; 1 Cor. 12; 14).

Objective Spirit

As a young student in 1925, Bonhoeffer's paper on the Holy Spirit defends the Lutheran principle of scriptural interpretation. Only God can understand God; therefore, only God the Holy Spirit can hear Scripture. All interpretation and preaching is a failure unless the Spirit is called upon to reveal what is written. Christ is alive and present as the Word of God from eternity. His appearance in verbal form is at the impetus of the Spirit in the written record, within which is Christ 'truly alive and present'.[49]

In a seminar paper in 1926, Bonhoeffer expounds on a fourfold pneumatological pattern found in Luther.[50] The first action of the Spirit is to activate awareness of sin with enormous 'convulsions of conscience' and a 'confrontation' between God and the human being bringing contrition.[51] The second action is to justify and sanctify the human being by faith so that possession of the Spirit is known by newness of life and works.[52] The third action is to impart faith so that Christ is grasped only through the medium of Scripture, 'the ultimate measuring stick and plumb line,' and not 'directly through some kind of special outpouring of the Holy Spirit'.[53] The fourth action is the Spirit's impact on the word of preaching in the outpouring at Pentecost and in the ongoing teaching and preaching of the church.

In *Sanctorum Communio* Bonhoeffer's conception of the Holy Spirit is developed along the lines of Hegelian philosophy.[54] Bonhoeffer understands the church to be a community of spirit, not an objective spirit in the Hegelian sense (a form of universal spirit whereby all individual life is absorbed into the corporate spirit, i.e. the Holy Spirit) but a purposive society which is the recipient of the divine will. He calls this a 'community of love' (*Liebesgemeinschaft*). For Bonhoeffer, the Holy Spirit is the objective spirit of the church, which means that, through intimate communion with the other, a 'community of will' or a collective person is established. The Holy Spirit brings us into unity with God. Thus when Christ comes into us through the Spirit, the church also comes into us in a double movement of love, upward to God and outward to others. Bonhoeffer does not make the mistake of equating the personality of the church with the Holy Spirit, but neither does he distinguish personal attributes of the Spirit apart from the community. He recognizes that the social relations of love are foundational in the formation of community, but does not apply this principle in any depth to Trinitarian relationships, although the doctrine of the Trinity is not neglected. An article, 'Concerning the Christian Idea of God', in *The Journal of Religion* (1932) was a commentary on the trisagion in Isaiah 6:3.[55]

The central feature in Bonhoeffer, which more often than not goes unremarked, is that Christ is the gift brought by the Spirit through preaching and service and that the guidance and resolution of ethical situations is the domain of the Spirit: 'The church community has to trust the Holy Spirit in every decision and believe strongly that the Spirit continues to be present in the community and at work in it'.[56] His belief in the prophetic dimension of moral leadership as the task of the Spirit, enabling the church to make true and right moral judgements, leads him to declare on 25 January 1936: 'I now believe that the Holy Ghost spoke at the synods of Barmen and Dahlem, which bound themselves to Scripture and confession alone . . . We can no longer free ourselves from the directing of the Holy Spirit'.[57]

At a Whitsun meeting in the Finkenwalde seminary, Bonhoeffer discourages the anticipation of further 'outpourings'. One of the students remembers that 'a third prayed for something special', while Bonhoeffer 'barred all hopes for a new miracle', as it was not a 'day of special inspiration, but it became a day of knowledge instead, calling us to faithful service in everyday matters and to obedient action'.[58] For Bonhoeffer the gift of tongues is not an unintelligible language of the Spirit which comes in 'stuttering and stammering'. It is a universal language of God and human togetherness to overcome misunderstanding and to promote responsibility.[59] The mark of the Pentecostal Spirit is love (*caritas*): 'even today Pentecost exists in all places where the *love* of Jesus is found'.[60] The Tegel theology unpacks these Whitsun remarks and demonstrates once again the centrality of Christ, who is all in all, in Bonhoeffer's creative speculations and analyses of the times.

A wide-angled lens

On 5 April 1943 Bonhoeffer was sent to Tegel prison charged with subverting the armed forces and on 8 October 1944 he was removed to the Gestapo prison at Prinz-Albrecht-Strasse. On 7 February 1945 he was sent to Buchenwald concentration camp and then moved to Regensburg. On 5 April his execution was ordered at Hitler's midday conference. On 6 April he was moved to Schönberg; on 8 April to Flossenbürg; and on 9 April, following a night-time summary court martial, he was executed by hanging, together with Oster, Sack, Canaris, Strünck and Gehre, part of the German military and government resistance plotting to overthrow Hitler.

Bonhoeffer's fragmentary reflections during his two-year imprisonment, published posthumously as *Letters and Papers from Prison*, have teased and baffled theologians for half a century. They are not disjointed abstractions but a continuum which follows a trajectory from the early and middle periods as he tries to earth the business of revelation in order that the Word may be 'haveable' and 'graspable' in the church and in the world. His abiding concern, 'Who is Christ for us today?', explores the question of how Christ can become a different reality, Lord of the world. It is to this end that he thinks along with the philosophers during the penultimate phase of his life. He ponders the progress of an autonomous world which can live without God as a stop-gap for unanswered questions. He worries about how to interpret the Bible in a non-religious and worldly way so as to make sense of justification, sanctification and rebirth.

The death of God

The flurry of analyses of Bonhoeffer's notions was sparked by the English bishop John Robinson and the 'Honest to God' debate of 1963, and dominated by British and American publications. Influential writers and theologians, for example, the imaginative and entertaining American professor Harvey Cox, drew Bonhoeffer into forms of secular Christianity. On both sides of the Atlantic death-of-God thinkers or Godless Christian thinkers denounced organized Christianity as an idolatry of irrelevant and outmoded cultural forms. In 1965 John T. Elson, the religion cover story writer for *Time* magazine, allied these secular philosophers with Bonhoeffer:

> [And] they follow closely in the footsteps of Dietrich Bonhoeffer, the anti-Nazi German martyr of World War II whose prison-cell writings speak of the need for the church to develop a 'non-religious interpretation of Biblical concepts', and of a secular world 'come of age' that no longer finds God necessary as a hypothesis to explain the sun and stars or as an answer to man's anxiety.

In 1966 Bonhoeffer is proposed as the secular guru whose focus on Jesus as 'the Man for others' implied the preaching of a spiritual hero for whom even non-Christians may have an admiration.[61]

Interpretations which attempt to read into Bonhoeffer the notion of a 'secular Christ' do not do justice to his assumptions of 'religion-less Christianity' nor to their philosophical roots. It is to Bonhoeffer's colonizing of the philosophers that we must once again turn in order to understand his thought processes in the final stage of his life. Unlike Hildegard's supernatural *visio*, we note in Bonhoeffer the attention to this world and its troubles, encapsulated tellingly in the term 'this-worldliness'.

This-worldliness

The German scholar Ralf Wüstenberg summarizes scholarship to date on the issue of philosophical streams and convincingly concludes that Bonhoeffer's analysis of modernity takes its bearings from the *Lebensphilosophie* (philosophy of life) of Wilhelm Dilthey (1833–1911), who highly influenced his point of view in 1944.[62] Bonhoeffer's project is to go far beyond the Barthian dialectic (the division of faith and the world) and further than the intention of faith as a new reality (a new inwardness or pietism), in order to embrace *life* and to relate it to Jesus Christ. As a *philosopher of life* Dilthey has the method with which to relate Christ to *life that has come of age.* How to relate *Jesus Christ to mature life* is the essence of Bonhoeffer's question, 'Who is Christ for us today?' On this basis, Bonhoeffer's radical programme is 'being for others', so that 'participation in Jesus' is 'to live as to believe' with a 'profound this-worldliness' in every aspect of worldly life. Bonhoeffer's 'ecclesiological conclusion' is that the churches must tell of what it means to live for Christ, to exist for others.[63] This point is spelt out, albeit in brief, in the abbreviated notes, 'Outline for a Book', which constitute a prophetic challenge to a church in a state of slumber. Bonhoeffer elaborates on a new way of thinking about church as an observer outside the church. The notes are ordered along the lines of God and the secular, and are pointers for the contemporary church on how to live in the world as Christians. Life in God is 'existence for others'; the transcendental is not the infinite and unattainable task but the neighbour who is within reach in any given situation. 'God in human form' is 'the man for others', recognizable as 'the Crucified, the man who lives out of the transcendent'. The task for a secular interpretation of the gospel is to discover the real meaning of Christian faith,

without evading the difficult questions, and without entrench-
ment behind 'the faith of the church'.[64]

For Bonhoeffer's turning point in his adaptation of new philosophical ideas in 1931 at the Union Theological Seminary, we
must look to the 'pragmatism' of William James, whose works he
read from start to finish. James postulates that if religion is true it
has meaning in life, but if it has no meaning in life then it is false.
It is probably his premise which fed the idea of earthbound pragmatism as a philosophy of life in Bonhoeffer's later thought.[65]
Bonhoeffer's ideal is to relate Jesus Christ to all the dimensions of
life. Jesus said, 'I have come so that they may have life and have
it to the full' (John 10:10). To take this statement and to apply it in
every respect is the vision behind 'this-worldliness' and Bonhoeffer's challenge to the church to live in the reality of this world.
Two aspects from his reading of Dilthey have direct bearing on
the prophetic Spirit: firstly, the view of this-worldly resurrection,
and, secondly, this-worldly speech about God.

This-worldly resurrection

In the letters and papers from Tegel prison, the relation between
resurrection and 'this-worldliness' contrasts fairly sharply with
the consistent view in the rest of the corpus that resurrection is an
historical event and everlasting life.[66] From prison Bonhoeffer critiques the resurrection hope which lies 'on the far side of the
boundary drawn by death'. On the contrary, resurrection 'sends
a man back to his life on earth in a wholly new way which is even
more sharply defined than it is in the Old Testament'. The
redemptions referred to in the Old Testament are '*historical*, i.e. on
this side of death'.[67] The essence of resurrection is this-worldly
transcendence: 'God is the beyond in the midst of our life'.[68] The
conception of God 'who wins power and space in the world by
his weakness', Bonhoeffer states, 'will probably be the starting-
point for our "secular interpretation"'.[69]

The problem with this view of resurrection is Christ, held *only*
in the worldly present and not in tension with the coming future.
There is no apparent dialectic, therefore, between the advents of
Christ's coming and his coming again, or between incarnation
and eschatology (the end things), as we found in Hildegard. The
thread between the penultimate (life on earth) and the ultimate

(life as it is to come) is a tenuous one. The need of hope for the present journey, for the future or for the end of life, which is the dominion of the Holy Spirit, mediator of comfort, is not accounted for ('and hope does not disappoint us, because God's love has been poured into our hearts through the Holy Spirit,' Romans 5:5). An historical assessment of religion, which has its roots in a vision of 'everydayness', falls prey to pragmatism, 'doing good', problem solving or self-sufficient programmatic ethics which have no need of the prayer, *Veni creator Spiritus*.

This-worldly speech

The astonishing simplicity of Bonhoeffer is his isolation of the problem of gospel communication to a world which manages without God: 'How do we speak of God – without religion, i.e. without the temporally conditioned presuppositions of metaphysics, inwardness, and so on? How do we speak (or perhaps we cannot even now "speak" as we used to) in a "secular" way about "God"?'[70] He asks how we speak in a 'worldly' sense about God and wants to move people from self-absorption with personal salvation to the greater matters of the day, a shocking agenda for a narcissistic religious age.[71] In a prophetic projection of the times he proposes a new language:

> It is not for us to prophesy the day (though the day will come) when men will once more be called so to utter the word of God that the world will be changed and renewed by it. It will be a new language, perhaps quite non-religious, but liberating and redeeming – as was Jesus' language; it will shock people and yet overcome them by its power.[72]

Lest we worry unnecessarily, we may be confident that Bonhoeffer is not advocating a conscious modernization or secularization of terminology, dogma or liturgy, nor a liberal reformist proposal to exchange the harshness of biblical vocabulary for a palatable message.[73] He sees the necessity of waiting for the word in a wordless silence until the times permit speech again. Bonhoeffer's vision continues to be resourced for fresh examinations of the word of God by individuals and groups who struggle, for instance, with oppressive regimes or who are seeking ways of gospel communication in a technologically advanced age. He is not a humanist who rejects faith, the supernatural, divine texts or the miraculous. He is not trying to work the world into a better place by faith in people and not in God. He believes in life after death; he loves life *before* death; ultimately his trust is in God. The prison doctor who attended him at the end wrote: 'I was most deeply moved by the way this extraordinary, lovable man prayed, so resigned and so certain that God heard his prayer'.[74]

However, Bonhoeffer's diagnosis of the times and his deducing of a new language for moderns pose a dilemma. Keeping the Bible for 'insiders' within the community of faith, and doing without it for 'outsiders', prohibits those outside from entering the hermeneutic circle and engaging with Christ, the prophetic subject matter of the biblical text. To allow the unfettered Word to speak in whichever way the prophetic Spirit chooses is to have the message infused with renewing power to the 'testimony of Jesus'. Here the mysteries of God are discerned by the Spirit (1 Cor. 2:10–16) and the redeeming love and purposes of Christ are retold anew for each generation (John 16:12–15). Hildegard's sermons and letters were addressed to insiders, persons who were either well within the Catholic Church or at the very least on its fringes. It is an interesting question to consider whether she would be as straightforward to outsiders on matters of faith, if born into a postmodern era of eclectic spiritualities and denominations. My hunch is that the anointing of the prophetic Spirit would propel her in exactly the same way to speak the truth, although her language would be up-to-date and relevant.

Illusive Spirit

John Zizioulas, a Greek Orthodox theologian, puts his finger on the problem of the subject of relating the work of Christ to the Holy Spirit in Bonhoeffer. He notes that for Bonhoeffer the Spirit is merely an assistant to bridge the distance between Christ and ourselves. The Spirit is not an agent who acts to facilitate Christ's presence in community in a day-by-day bond of ministry. The concept that Christ died 'for me' is a key term in Bonhoeffer (see especially *GS* III, 166, p. 242). This idea is not, however, applied to the Spirit. The Spirit is not a helper to make Christ real in the believer. The Spirit makes present today what Christ did on earth then. Zizioulas puts it thus: 'What, therefore, the Spirit does through the ministry is to constitute the Body of Christ *here and now* by *realizing* Christ's ministry *as* the Church's ministry'.[75] Although Bonhoeffer discusses the image of Christ in the believer as the work of the Trinity in general, he fails to demonstrate the operations of the Spirit in particular: 'It is indeed the holy Trinity who dwells within Christians, who permeates them and changes them into the very image of the triune God'.[76]

Personal Spirit retrieved

An examination of Luther's notion of the Spirit as 'infusion of love' (*infusio caritatis*) guides us out of the cul de sac in Bonhoeffer. Elements which advance the operations of the Spirit in a prophetical way may be retrieved from Luther. Although Luther was an Augustinian monk, Hildegard stood in the same general monastic tradition and we are right to assume that in both writers the operations of the Spirit are directly expressed and personally experienced. Regin Prenter, a Danish Lutheran priest and theologian, who was active in the resistance against the Nazi movement, shows that Luther reworks the abstract *caritas* (love) scheme into a realistic view of the Spirit.[77] Luther exegetes Romans 2:15 thus: 'Therefore I believe that the sentence, "The law is written on their hearts", is the same as "God's love has been poured ['is infused'] into our hearts through the Holy Spirit" (Rom. 5:5)'.[78]

The first action of the Spirit in Luther's fourfold scheme, described above, is to foster an awareness of sin. Here there is trust in a personal Spirit who prays in the same way as Christ prays (Heb. 7:25): 'It is the Spirit of the body of Christ, and helps the saints in their weaknesses, groaning and interceding for them'.[79] The groans of the Spirit are an 'infusion of love' as he enters the darkness of human distress as helper and burden-bearer: 'Therefore, when everything is hopeless for us and all things begin to go against our prayers and desires, then those unutterable groans begin. And then "the Spirit helps us in our weakness" (Rom. 8:26). For unless the Spirit were helping, it would be impossible for us to bear this action of God by which he hears us and accomplishes what we pray for.'[80]

The second action of the Spirit is as sanctifier and transformer of the soul, pouring into hearts the love of Christ (Rom. 5:5), and, through mortification and regeneration, conforming the soul to Christ. Prenter shows that this is not a human struggle, but one accomplished by the Spirit. He explains that for Luther there can be no synthesis of the Spirit of God and the spirit of man, but rather a confrontation of 'an offensive realism in the witness of the Spirit'. Neither is the personal being of the Spirit in Luther more or less dissolved in the being of the Father and Son.[81]

The third action of the Spirit is to make Christ present in the Bible. Luther's commentary on Romans underlines the dynamic of an outpouring or infusion of the Spirit upon the written word of the Bible to make present the Spirit so that the resurrection of Christ may be proclaimed. The Spirit works, therefore, to present Christ in the outward word just as much as he was in the Jesus of the flesh. The Spirit alone contemporizes and transforms Scripture into a saving word.[82]

The fourth action in Luther is the infusion of the Spirit in preaching. His exegesis of the text Matthew 11:15 highlights the necessity of the Spirit in effecting any change at all in the listeners: '[The] Word of God is not heard even among adults and those who hear unless the Spirit promotes growth inwardly. Accordingly, it is a word of power and grace when it infuses the Spirit at the same time that it strikes the ears. But if it does not infuse the Spirit, then he who hears does not differ at all from one who is deaf'.[83] The sovereignty of the Spirit in proclamation applies as acutely to the prophet, who becomes a mouthpiece, entitled to operate only with a divine unction: 'You can openly proclaim out of the fullness of your heart and spirit, but you cannot openly pour out the Spirit himself, nor can you infuse him and so make others feel the feeling you have'.[84]

The desire of Bonhoeffer is the making present of Christ. Luther's fourfold action plan helps to make Christ present in a decisive way. For example, when the Spirit as interlocutor prays on behalf of the saints (Rom. 8:26–27), we are reminded of Christ who intercedes at the right hand of the Father (Heb. 7:25). This is a mission common to both the Son and the Spirit. When the person of the Spirit is tangibly present in the *Anfechtung* and temptations of the disciple with 'sighs too deep for words' (Rom. 8:26), then we are reminded of the task to stand with Christ at the cross. In Luther's commentary on Genesis 1:2 we are shown that one of the 'offices' of the Spirit is to make alive, to create from nothing (*ex nihilo*). The Spirit's 'mothering' of creation nurtures universal new life. Likewise, the Spirit can coax into life and bring into being the things we need for the entire mission of the church, if we will but ask: 'As a hen broods her eggs, keeping them warm, in order to hatch her chicks, and, as it were, to bring them to life through heat, so scripture says that the Holy Spirit brooded, as it were, on the waters to bring to life those substances which were to be quickened and adorned. For it is the office of the Holy Spirit to make alive.'[85]

Faces Unveiled

> Now the Lord is the Spirit, and where the Spirit of the Lord is, there is freedom. And all of us, with unveiled faces, seeing the glory of the Lord as though reflected in a mirror, are being transformed into the same image from one degree of glory to another; for this comes from the Lord, the Spirit (2 Cor. 3:17–18).

In this chapter we have tracked with two visionaries who are poles apart. Understandably our question will be, so what does this all mean for us today? Hildegard is out of the ordinary; her pictures are strange and may bemuse us. We have to agree, however, that the Spirit in Hildegard is not simply a multiplication sign making up the numerical equation of the Trinity, thus 1x1 or Father and Son joined by the Spirit = Trinity. Such mathematical logic shrinks the 'hand' of the Holy Spirit. In Hildegard the Spirit is not merely an invisible and extraneous multiplication sign but *the* positive and essential person who adds vigour to the Christian's life. Hildegard's doctrine of the Spirit reflects true medieval inseparability and reinforces the ever-present bond of love of the Spirit in the notion of *personaliter*. The person of the Spirit is very much a singular and significant part of the communal make-up of the Trinity. Without the Spirit, the work of Christ cannot be effective in transfiguring the soul. In the prophet's life the Spirit is a challenging force, a striking and compelling charism, a strong 'hand' grasping and laying hold of the mind, imagination, emotion and will. Fumbling in philosophical fields for answers to dilemmas cannot replace the precision of the Spirit's gift in laying bare the soul of the world and infusing it with the lively word of the Lord. However persuasive Bonhoeffer's argument about the world come of age, it has to be said that it does not say enough. Transformation is a direct work of the Holy Spirit. To draw upon patristic-medieval pneumatology is to dig deep into a treasure house filled with precious nuggets of truth to enhance contemporary prophecy.

At the close of this chapter there are two areas which we as leaders are obliged to face. Firstly, if indeed the church has gained or lost in spiritual force as she has upheld passionately or lukewarmly the doctrine of the 'personality' of the Spirit, then a recovery of the person of the Spirit, in our theology and practice, is not an optional extra but a vital necessity to safeguard the church's well-being.[86] Secondly, if the door to heavenly vision is to be kept open not just a crack, but wide open, it is incumbent upon the church to engage with the 'Spirit of prophecy', not as a background murmur but in the forefront of everything we do. To live life in all its fullness requires the supernatural help of the Spirit to pull it off. Dreaming with God can be fruitless without the freedom the Spirit brings. This is not only of scholarly interest or vague pastoral concern but is the essence of progressive ministry in the area of prophecy. To lift up our eyes to the hills from whence cometh our help is pretty pointless as an abstract; but, as directed to the person of the Holy Spirit, it is powerful. As church practitioners, therefore, we will have to come to terms with the problematic of the visionary and dreamer. Instead of holding such people at arm's length, rather hoping that they will hop off to other churches, should we not seek a way forward to incorporate them into the worshipping life of the congregation? Will conversation with them to assess their contribution, with church members trained in these matters, not assist in the discernment of their offerings and enrich our worship and life together?

CONCLUSION

We have come to the end of a very cursory examination of Hildegard of Bingen and Dietrich Bonhoeffer, which cannot do justice to the measure of their greatness. However, at the interface of their lives and works we have tried to engage with some of the meatier portions of prophecy: the relationship between the individual prophet and the church; matters of authenticity and authority; searching Scripture prophetically; preaching and teaching prophetically; reading Christ as the endpoint of Scripture; the charismatic gift of the Holy Spirit; the bond between the 'testimony of Jesus' and the 'Spirit of prophecy'; the acceptance of the persons of both Jesus Christ and the Holy Spirit as a necessity, and not an optional extra, for the full release of prophetic utterance. In these chapters we have visited two centuries and two worldviews, using our keys as permits of travel to unlock the doors into their treasure houses: guides to the supernatural, Jesus in Scripture, 3-D cosmic vision, play on words and pictorial language, the Man for others, community of the cross, the way of mysticism, the way of powerlessness, the way of death, minorities of one, call for courage, seers, dreams, public responsibility, private prayer, commitment to the task, leadership, and the Spirit. And questions arise. Was the journey not simply the one we have made many times before – the route of *either* personal piety (Hildegard) *or* social activism (Bonhoeffer)? The wild geese have it right – *one* leader at a time in formation lets me off the hook – for now and forever. Is this right thinking or wrong-headedness?

In this work I have attempted to correlate the vision and thinking of two extremely powerful prophetic leaders. In a nutshell I have suggested that prophecy is best understood as a union between two irreducible norms, that is, the testimony of Jesus Christ, the Word of God, and the supernatural presence of the gift of the Holy Spirit. Put another way, I have attempted to argue that the two spiritual traditions regarding Word and Spirit, which are represented by Hildegard and Bonhoeffer, point the way to a more complete rendering of the gift of prophecy than if only one path were to be considered.

The survey cannot by any stretch of the imagination pretend to be a comprehensive systematic study of church prophecy. It has not dealt with the situation of the church, in its wider sense, being a prophetic people, or the community of prophets rather than the lone person. It has simply flagged up ideas to be used in forums of discussion and debate, or for private contemplation. By nature of being a book about prophecy, it must consider the future.

At the turn of the third millennium our thoughts turned upon the future. We gazed ahead to speculate and consider where the world would be in 2010. We have arrived there now and the likelihood is that we feel none the wiser. The global economy is predictably uncertain, the rich are richer and the poor poorer. Nations still pick up weapons against nations and the wolf does not lie down with the lamb. We search the skies for answers and hear our own voices echoing in the vast drum of a cosmic landscape. Hollowness, randomness and alienation are the plague even of the finest systems of internet sociability – 800 million Facebook users (and growing) do little to heal the acne of blemished relationships. If we are honest, the world is too much with us, surrounded as we are at every waking hour by politicians, celebrities, style gurus, iPhone, headset, me-time, you-time, us-time, schedules past, present and future. Our analyses of our times are unremarkable and available online at all times. We read much and yet seem to know little about God, apart from what others say. Or is this pessimism at its worst? Is the world in fact improving and evolving? Are we becoming nicer and more whole people? Is God still with us? Is he coming again? How soon? Or does he come in the little advents of daily life? Should we be content with the small signs? Has he come again in Swedenborgianism or transcendentalism, Scientology, Christian

Science, channelling, the Jehovah's Witnesses, the Quakers, the levitators, the street people, the protestors, save the whale, the Nobel prize winners, the nameless, faceless others? Where is Jesus now? Who is Jesus for us today?

The political philosopher Michael Sandel, professor of government at Harvard University, is the teacher of the highly acclaimed lecture course, 'Justice: What's the Right Thing To Do?', which is delivered to 1,200 students and available as a series of twelve public episodes on the web. His recent publication includes the topic of religion as a private matter without considering its bearing on public responsibilities. He uses the American president, Barack Obama, as an example of a religious conscience helping to shape the common good of a nation.[1]

Before the presidential election, and in his introductory remarks in the Call to Renewal Keynote Address on 28 June 2006 in Washington DC, Barack Obama stated his intention to discuss the connection between religion and politics. He explained that America is a pluralist society and that he had acted in accordance with the liberal way of affirming all views without taking sides and imposing his own beliefs. But he had now come to believe that it was a mistake to 'abandon the field of religious discourse'. He went on to speak about a religious 'tendency' and a 'hunger' in the American people, which goes beyond causes or religious marketing, and is a moral and spiritual 'yearning', an acknowledgement that something is missing, a need for purpose and a 'narrative arc' to their lives. Obama suggested that American people are religious and that 'secularists are wrong when they ask believers to leave their religion at the door before entering into the public square'. He went on to argue that the majority of the great reformers (for example, Abraham Lincoln and Martin Luther King) were driven by faith and used religious language to win their causes. Not to insert 'personal morality' into policy debates is absurd, given that much of the law is grounded on the Judeo-Christian tradition. As a South African, I was intrigued to note a similar sentiment expressed by a South African journalist in a daily newspaper at the outset of 2011. These are stirring words uncovering the spiritual core of a nation whose feeling for the future is generally upbeat and driven by the impetus of forward thinking in most aspects of national life: 'When I look back at the past year I am struck by the huge emptiness at the centre of our national discourse and our being'.[2]

Even in a moral sense Sandel and Obama are stressing the fact that religion is not only vertical, but horizontal, and that there is an imperative to find both the upward and the outward dimensions. The way of being a lover of God and at the same time a lover of the other is the single path offered by a synthesis of Hildegard and Bonhoeffer. On the one hand, we are called to abandon ourselves and all riches for the love of God; on the other we are asked to love our neighbour as we do ourselves. Keeping a bifocal vision will purify a humanitarian sentiment, driven at times less by passion for Christ, and more by doing the good thing. Jesus' response to the wealthy young ruler that 'no one is good but God' is a particular nugget of wisdom to temper the strivings of an overworked conscience. Goodness, too, is a slippery road to introspection and self-improvement, unless safeguarded by the moral horizon of a greater word, that of the Christian Scriptures. It has to be the Christian Scriptures if we are discussing Christian prophecy, although I remain convinced that God may choose to speak in any other way he likes. For our purposes, however, the Bible is the highway and we are people of the book.

The rather bleak landscape I painted in the opening remarks of this work intimated that prophecy is scarce. The word of God is, however, not difficult to find. The commandment is close at hand, not in an awkward unassailable bulwark in heaven, fiercely guarded by a battalion of the angelic host, to be released at the command of the next tablet-bearing guru; nor in an impregnable fortress in the abyss, locked in by the powers of daemon, from whom it must be wrested with great travail (cf. Deut. 30:11–14; Rom. 10:5–17). The Word is Jesus Christ, and his coming has been accomplished once for all. He is the key of David, who unlocks the treasures of the heights and the depths. His word stands for all time. He is the beginning and the end of Scripture and he unrolls the scroll of the future. He is the interpreter of Scripture and its most accomplished exegete. If the word of Christ is in our mouths, and the Spirit is the pulsation that impels its truth, then both persons are close at hand ready and willing to unpack the word for our lives, our nation and our world. By means of the hands of

Jesus and the Spirit present at *our* right hand, we may with confidence read the signs of the times.

In a few closing remarks I would like to highlight three aspects that I think are important as we project ourselves and those near and dear (church families, parishes, ministries and national focus) into a futuristic landscape. I propose that they are held together in a Trinitarian threefold knot and not disentangled: supernatural vision given straight from God, through the authority of Jesus Christ, and in the anointing and power of the Holy Spirit. This is not an abstract formula without significant content. Each of the three persons must be included as such, as person, with everything pertaining to *personaliter*. The three-way test is a safety net to catch ones falling into the trap of giving false prophecy or of receiving it:

> If prophets or those who divine by dreams appear among you and promise you omens or portents, and the omens or the portents declared by them take place, and they say, 'Let us follow other gods' (whom you have not known) 'and let us serve them', you must not heed the words of those prophets or those who divine by dreams; for the Lord your God is testing you, to know whether you indeed love the Lord your God with all your heart and soul (Deut. 13:1–5).

Each of the three scenarios occurs in relation to the icon *Trinity*, by the medieval Russian Orthodox Andrei Rublev (1370–1430). An icon is a piece of wood with a painted representation of some spiritual truth, in this case the visitation of the three angels to Abraham at the oaks of Mamre (Gen. 18:1–15), as a visible foreshadowing of the three persons of the Holy Trinity. The reader may recall that a brief mention of this biblical text was made in the exposition of the Trinity in Hildegard in Chapter 3. Over the years, the icon is held, kissed and touched as a meeting point with God. Tears and fears are in the fabric of its design; thoughts and prayers ascend from its surface. The wood in itself is unspiritual; it is not an idol. The iconographer is a paintbrush in God's hand. Rublev painted the masterpiece as a touching place between heaven and earth. We consider it in three ways as we try to predict or assess our times against the background of *Trinity* and the monstrous, violent enslavement of the Russian people under the Tartar Yoke (1382–1448).

Without vision people perish
Rublev is a luminary seer who sees more clearly than most the need of his people for the upward gaze. In an epiphanous time of meditation and inspiration he paints a prayer for all time of a heavenly reality. The earthly terror of the Tatar-Mongul domination is transcended in the icon by an invitation to be drawn into the infinite dimension of heaven's feast. The meal of hospitality with friends is at once a familiar affair such as may be experienced in finite life on earth, and an expression of the infinite hope of eternity and the banquet to come. *Trinity* restores future hope. It is a place to touch God in the present for mercy and faith again for the future.

And the Word became flesh and dwelt among us
The Word is the first of the 'double agents' in Orthodoxy. Jesus Christ is the Word himself but he is also the expositor of the written word of the Scriptures. He is at one and the same time the exegete and the exegesis of Scripture. Without him nothing was created and he is life in the present and into eternity. As we kiss the Son (Ps. 2:12) in worship, we find the truth for our lives because he is Truth.

The Spirit gives life; the flesh is useless
The palpable presence of the Holy Spirit is the second of the 'double agents'. He *is* the Gift of God in prayers and supplications – with or without tangible gifts of graces of the streams of church traditions: tongues, signs and wonders; icons, flowing robes, unseen priests; beads, masses and liturgies. The Spirit is the custodian of all the tradition of the church that has passed since the day of Pentecost, and the gateway to all the resourceful hope for the future.

Shall we find wisdom for today? Like sunlight, wisdom is unbound and free. All the books in the world, all the human thinking, cannot replace God's wisdom, a gift from above. James, the writer of the epistle, put it thus: 'Any of you who lacks wisdom must ask God, who gives to all generously and without scolding; it will be given' (James 1:5, *The New Jerusalem Bible*).

BIBLIOGRAPHY

Hildegard of Bingen

(Abbrev. CCCM = Corpus Christianorum: continuatio mediaevalis)

Critical editions

Hildegard of Bingen. *Hildegard Bingensis Epistolarium*, CCCM (ed. Lieven van Acker, XCI – XCIA, ed. Lieven van Acker and Monika Klaes-Hachmöller, XCIB; Turnhout: Brepols, 1991–2001).
—. *Hildegard Bingensis Liber Diuinorum Operum*, CCCM (ed. A. Derolez and P. Dronke; Turnhout: Brepols, 1996), XCII.
—. *Hildegard Bingensis Liber Vite Meritorum*, CCCM (ed. Angela Carlevaris; Turnhout: Brepols, 1995), XC.
—. *Hildegard Bingensis Scivias*, CCCM (ed. Adelgundis Führkötter and Angela Carlevaris; Turnhout: Brepols, 1978), XLIII–XLIIIA.
—. *Ordo Virtutum*, in *Nine Medieval Latin Plays* (ed. and trans. Peter Dronke; Cambridge: Cambridge University Press, 1994).
—. *Symphonia Armonie Celestium Revelationum* (ed. and trans. Barbara Newman; Ithaca, NY; London: Cornell University Press, 2nd edn, 1998).
—. *Symphonia Armonie Celestium Revelationum* (8 vols, ed. and trans. Marianne Richert Pfau; Bryn Mawr, PA: Hildegard Publishing Co., 1997).
—. *Symphonia Harmoniae Caelestium Revelationum*, Peter van Poucke, facsimile ed. of Dendermonde mss with music (Peer: Alamire, 1991).

Primary sources

Augustine of Hippo. *De Doctrina Christiana* (ed. J.-P. Migne; Paris, 1841), PL, XXXIV.

Gottfried of Disibodenberg and Theodoric of Echternach. *Vita Sanctae Hildegardis*, CCCM (ed. Monika Klaes, Turnhout: Brepols, 1993), CXXVI.

Guibert of Gembloux. *Guiberti Gemblacensis, Epistolae: Part 1, Epistolae 1–29*, CCCM (ed. Albert Derolez; Turnhout: Brepols, 1988), LXVIA.

Hildegard of Bingen. *Analecta Sanctae Hildegardis Opera Spicilegio Solesmensi Parata* in *Analecta Sacra Spicilegio Solesmensi* (ed. J.-B. Pitra; Farnborough: Gregg Press, 1966–67), VIII.

Rupert of Deutz. *R.D.D. Ruperti Opera Omnia* (ed. J.-P. Migne; Paris, 1854), PL, CLXVII-CLXX.

Translations of the works

Hildegard of Bingen. *Hildegard of Bingen: On Natural Philosophy and Medicine* (ed. and trans. Margaret Berger; Cambridge: D.S. Brewer, 1999).

-——. *Hildegard of Bingen's Book of Divine Works, with Letters and Songs* (ed. Matthew Fox, trans. Robert Cunningham; Sante Fe, NM: Bear & Co., 1987).

——. *Hildegard of Bingen: Selected Writings* (trans. Mark Atherton; London: Penguin, 2001).

——. *Scivias*, Classics of Western Spirituality (ed. and trans. Columba Hart and Jane Bishop; New York: Paulist Press, 1990).

——. *The Book of the Rewards of Life* (trans. Bruce W. Hozeski, Garland Library of Medieval Literature, Series B, vol. 89 (New York; London: Garland, 1994).

——. *The Letters of Hildegard of Bingen* (3 vols; ed. and trans. Joseph L. Baird and Radd K. Ehrman; Oxford: Oxford University Press, 1994–2004).

Silvas, Anna. *Jutta and Hildegard: The Biographical Sources,* Brepols Medieval Women Series (University Park: The Pennsylvania State University Press, 1999).

Secondary sources

Berndt, Rainer, ed. *'Im Angesicht Gottes suche der Menschen sich selbst': Hildegard von Bingen (1098–1179),* Erudiri Sapientia, II (Berlin: Akademie Verlag, 2001).

Burnett, Charles and Peter Dronke, eds. *Hildegard of Bingen: The Context of Her Thought and Art,* Warburg Institute Colloquia, 4 (London: Warburg Institute, 1998).

Dreyer, Elizabeth *A. Passionate Spirituality: Hildegard of Bingen and Hadewijch of Brabant* (New York: Paulist Press, 2005).

Dronke, Peter. *Women Writers of the Middle Ages: A Critical Study of Texts from Perpetua (+203) to Marguerite Porete (+1310)* (Cambridge: Cambridge University Press, 1984).

Kienzle, Beverly Mayne. *Hildegard of Bingen and Her Gospel Homilies: Speaking New Mysteries,* Medieval Women: Texts and Contexts, vol. 12 (Turnhout: Brepols, 2009).

Menzies, Lucy. *Mirrors of the Holy: Ten Studies in Sanctity* (London: A.R. Mowbray, 1928).

Newman, Barbara, ed. *Voice of the Living Light: Hildegard of Bingen and Her World* (Berkeley, CA; London: University of California Press, 1998).

—. 'Hildegard of Bingen: Visions and Validations', *Church History* 54 (1985): pp. 163–75.

Dietrich Bonhoeffer

Primary sources

Bonhoeffer, Dietrich. *Gesammelte Schriften* (5 vols; Munich: C. Kaiser, 1965–72)

Translations of the works

Bonhoeffer, Dietrich. *Act and Being* (ed. Wayne Whitson Floyd Jr., trans. by H. Martin Rumscheidt; Minneapolis: Fortress Press, 1996).

—. *A Testament to Freedom: The Essential Writings of Dietrich Bonhoeffer* (ed. Geffrey B. Kelly and F. Burton Nelson; San Francisco: HarperSanFrancisco, 1990).

—. *Creation and Fall* (ed. John W. de Gruchy, trans. Douglas Stephen Bax; Minneapolis: Fortress Press, 1997).

—. *Discipleship* (ed. Geffrey B. Kelly and John D. Godsey, trans. Barbara Green and Reinhard Krauss; Minneapolis: Fortress Press, 2001).

—. *Ethics* (ed. Clifford J. Green, trans. Reinhard Krauss, Charles C. West and Douglas W. Stott; Minneapolis: Fortress Press, 2005).

—. *Fiction from Tegel Prison* (ed. Clifford J. Green, trans. Nancy Lukens; Minneapolis: Fortress Press, 1999).

—. *Lectures on Christology* (trans. Edwin Robertson; London: Collins, 1978).

—. *Letters and Papers from Prison* (ed. Eberhard Bethge; London: SCM, enlarged edn, 1971)

—. *Life Together and Prayerbook of the Bible* (ed. Geffrey B. Kelly, trans. Daniel W. Bloesch and James H. Burtness; Minneapolis: Fortress Press, 1996).

—. *Meditating on the Word* (ed. and trans. David McI. Gracie (Cambridge, MA: Cowley, 1986).

—. *No Rusty Swords: Letters, Lectures and Notes 1928–1936 from the Collected Works of Dietrich Bonhoeffer*, I (trans. Edwin H. Robertson and John Bowden; London: Collins, 1965).

—. *Sanctorum Communio* (ed. Clifford J. Green, trans. Reinhard Krauss and Nancy Lukens; Minneapolis: Fortress Press, 1998).

—. *Spiritual Care* (trans. Jay C. Rochelle; Philadelphia: Fortress Press, 1985).

—. *The Way to Freedom: Letters, Lectures and Notes 1935–1939 from the Collected Works of Dietrich Bonhoeffer*, II (trans. Edwin H. Robertson and John Bowden; London: Collins, 1966).

—. *The Young Bonhoeffer, 1918–1927* (ed. Paul Duane Matheny, Clifford J. Green and Marshall D. Johnson, trans. Mary C. Nebelsick assisted by Douglas W. Stott; Minneapolis: Fortress Press, 2003).

Secondary sources

Bethge, Eberhard. *Dietrich Bonhoeffer: Theologian, Christian, Man for His Times* (rev. and ed. Victoria J. Barnett; Minneapolis: Fortress Press, 2000).

Feil, Ernst and Ilse Tödt, eds. *Konsequenzen: Dietrich Bonhoeffers Kirchenverständnis heute*, Internationales Bonhoeffer Forum, Forschung und Praxis, 3 (Munich: Kaiser, 1980).

Green, Clifford J. *Bonhoeffer: A Theology of Sociality* (Grand Rapids: Eerdmans, 1999).

Gregor, Brian and Jens Zimmermann, eds. *Bonhoeffer and Continental Thought: Cruciform Philosophy,* Indiana Series in the Philosophy of Religion (Bloomington: Indiana University Press, 2009).

Kelly, Geffrey B. and F. Burton Nelson. *The Cost of Moral Leadership: The Spirituality of Dietrich Bonhoeffer* (Grand Rapids; Cambridge: Eerdmans, 2003).

Lawrence, Joel. *Bonhoeffer: A Guide for the Perplexed* (London: T&T Clark International, 2010).

Quaintance, Susan. 'Dietrich Bonhoeffer and Benedictine Monasticism: *Life Together*', *The American Benedictine Review* 48 (1997): pp. 347–60.

Smith, Ronald Gregor, ed. *World Come of Age: A Symposium on Dietrich Bonhoeffer* (London: Collins, 1967).

Wannenwetsch, Bernd, ed. *Who Am I? Bonhoeffer's Theology through His Poetry* (London: T&T Clark, 2009).

Wüstenberg, Ralf K. *Glauben als Leben: Dietrich Bonhoeffer und die nichtreligiöse Interpretation biblischer Bergriffe* (Frankfurt am Main: P. Lang, 1996).

Zimmermann, Wolf-Dieter and Ronald Gregor Smith, eds. *I Knew Dietrich Bonhoeffer: Reminiscences by His Friends* (trans. Käthe Gregor Smith; London: Collins, 1966).

Related Texts

Anselm of Canterbury. *The Prayers and Meditations of St Anselm* (trans. Benedicta Ward; Harmondsworth: Penguin, 1973).

Augustine of Hippo. *Expositions on the Book of Psalms by Saint Augustin Bishop of Hippo*, A Select Library of the Nicene and Post-Nicene Fathers of the Christian Church, VIII (ed. A. Cleveland Coxe; Grand Rapids: Eerdmans, 1974).

—. *The Trinity*, The Fathers of the Church: A New Translation, XLV (trans. Stephen McKenna; Washington: The Catholic University of America Press, 1970).

Barth, Karl. *The Epistle to the Romans* (trans. from the 6th edn Edwyn H. Hoskyns; London: H. Milford, 1933).

—. *The Word of God and the Word of Man* (trans. Douglas Horton; London: Hodder & Stoughton, 1928).

Bede. *Ecclesiastical History of the English People, with Bede's Letter to Egberg and Cuthbert's Letter on the Death of Bede* (rev. and ed. R.E. Latham, trans. Leo Sherley-Price; London: Penguin Books, 1990).

Benedict of Nursia. *The Rule of St Benedict in English* (ed. Timothy Fry; The Liturgical Press: Collegeville, 1982).

Braaten, Carl E. and Robert W. Jensen, eds. *Reclaiming the Bible for the Church* (Edinburgh: T&T Clark, 1995).

Brueggemann, Walter. *Theology of the Old Testament: Testimony, Dispute, Advocacy* (Minneapolis: Fortress Press, 1997).

Childs, Brevard S. 'Toward Recovering Theological Exegesis', *Ex Auditu* 16 (2000): pp. 121–9.

Cunningham, Conor and Peter M. Candler, eds. *Belief and Metaphysics* (London: SCM, 2007).

Dronke, Peter. *Poetic Individuality in the Middle Ages: New Departures in Poetry 1000–1150* (Oxford: Clarendon Press, 1970).

—. *The Medieval Lyric* (London: Hutchinson, 2nd edn, 1978).

Ebeling, Gerhard. *Word and Faith* (trans. J.C.B. Mohr; London: SCM Press, 1st English edn, 1963).

Elson, John T. 'Theology', *Time* 86.17 (1965): pp. 62–3.

—. 'Is God Dead?' *Time* 87.14 (1966): pp. 50–54.

Evans, G.R. *The Thought of Gregory the Great* (Cambridge: Cambridge University Press, 1986).

Farrer, Austin. *The Glass of Vision*, Bampton Lectures, 1948 (Westminster: Dacre Press, 1948).

Feuerbach, Ludwig. *Lectures on the Essence of Religion* (trans. Ralph Manheim; New York: Harper & Row, 1967).

—. *The Essence of Christianity* (trans. George Eliot; New York: Harper & Brothers Publishers, 1957).

Harmless, William. *Mystics* (New York: Oxford University Press, 2008).

Hegel, Georg Wilhelm Friedrich. *Lectures on the Philosophy of Religion: The Consummate Religion*, III (ed. Peter C. Hodgson, R.F. Brown and others; Berkeley; London: University of California Press, 1985).

—. *Phenomenology of Spirit* (trans. A.V. Miller, analysis of text J.N. Findlay; Oxford: Clarendon Press, 1997).

Herbert, A.G. *The Throne of David: A Study of the Fulfilment of the Old Testament in Jesus Christ and His Church* (London: Faber & Faber, 1941).

Hopkins, Gerard Manley. *Poems and Prose of Gerard Manley Hopkins* (ed. W.H. Gardner; Harmondsworth: Penguin, 1953).

Hunter, James Davison. *To Change the World: The Irony, Tragedy, and Possibility of Christianity in the Late Modern World* (New York: Oxford University Press, 2010).

James, William. *The Varieties of Religious Experience: A Study in Human Nature, Being the Gifford Lectures on Natural Religion Delivered at Edinburgh in 1901–1902* (London: Longmans, Green, and Co., 1915).

John Cassian. *John Cassian: The Conferences,* Ancient Christian Writers, The Works of the Fathers in Translation, LVII (trans. Boniface Ramsey; New York: Paulist Press, 1997).

John of Salisbury. *Frivolities of Courtiers and Footprints of Philosophers: A Translation of Books I, II, III and Selections from Books VII and VIII of the Policraticus* (trans. Joseph B. Pike; London, H. Milford: Oxford University Press, 1938).

Justin Martyr. *Justin, Philosopher and Martyr: Apologies* (ed. with commentary on the text Denis Minns and Paul Parvis; Oxford: Oxford University Press, 2009).

Kelly, J.N.D. *A Commentary on the Epistles of Peter and of Jude* (London: A. & C. Black, 1969).

Kempis, Thomas à. *The Imitation of Christ* (rev. Harold J. Chadwick; Nashville, 1999).

Kienzle, Beverly Mayne. *Cistercians, Heresy and Crusade in Occitania, 1145–1229: Preaching in the Lord's Vineyard* (Woodbridge: York Medieval Press, 2001).

Knight, Jonathan. *2 Peter and Jude*, New Testament Guides (Sheffield: Sheffield Academic Press, 1995).

Kruger, S.F. *Dreaming in the Middle Ages* (Cambridge: Cambridge University Press, 1992).

Leclercq, Jean. *The Love of Learning and the Desire for God: A Study of Monastic Culture* (trans. C. Misrahi; New York: Fordham University Press, 1974).

Lewis, C.S. *The Allegory of Love: A Study in Medieval Tradition* (Oxford: Oxford University Press, 1958).

Lewis-Williams, David. *Conceiving God: The Cognitive Origin and Evolution of Religion* (London: Thomas & Hudson, 2010).

Louth, Andrew. *Discerning the Mystery: An Essay on the Nature of Theology* (Oxford: Clarendon Press, 1983).

Lubac, Henri de. *Catholicism: A Study of Dogma in Relation to the Corporate Destiny of Mankind* (trans. Lancelot C. Sheppard; London: Burns, Oates & Washbourne, 1950).

—. *Medieval Exegesis: The Four Senses of Scripture* (2 vols, trans. Mark Sebanc; Edinburgh: T&T Clark, 1998–2000).

—. *The Discovery of God* (trans. Alexander Dru, notes trans. Mark Sebanc and Cassian Fulsom; Edinburgh: T&T Clark, 1996).

—. *The Drama of Atheist Humanism* (trans. Edith M. Riley; London: Sheed & Ward, 1949).

—. *The Mystery of the Supernatural* (trans. Rosemary Sheed; London: G. Chapman, 1967).

Luther, Martin. LW, XXXII, *Career of the Reformer* II (ed. George W. Forell; Philadelphia: Fortress Press, 1958).

—. LW, X, *First Lectures on the Psalms I, Psalms 1 – 75* (ed. Hilton C. Oswald; St Louis: Concordia Publishing House, 1974).

—. LW, XXVII, *Lectures on Galatians 1535: Chapters 5 – 6, Lectures on Galatians 1519: Chapters 1 – 6* (ed. Jaroslav Pelikan; St Louis: Concordia Publishing House, 1964).

—. LW, I, *Lectures on Genesis: Chapters 1 – 5* (ed. Jaroslav Pelikan; St Louis: Concordia Publishing House, 1958).

—. LW, XXV, *Lectures on Romans: Glosses and Scholia* (ed. Hilton C. Oswald; St Louis: Concordia Publishing House, 1972).

—. LW, XXII, *Sermons on the Gospel of St John: Chapters 1 – 4* (ed. Jaroslav Pelikan; St Louis: Concordia Publishing House, 1957).

Malala, Justice. 'SA needs visionary at the helm', *The Times*, 10 January 2011, p. 8.

McCracken, G.E. and A. Cabaniss, eds. *Early Medieval Theology*, The Library of Christian Classics, IX (London: SCM, 1957).

McGrath, Alister E. *Luther's Theology of the Cross: Martin Luther's Theological Breakthrough* (Oxford: Blackwell, 1985).

Milbank, John. *The Suspended Middle: Henri de Lubac and the Debate concerning the Supernatural* (Grand Rapids: Eerdmans, 2005).

Muessig, Carolyn and Ad Putter, eds. *Envisaging Heaven in the Middle Ages,* Routledge Studies in Medieval Religion and Culture (Oxford: Routledge, 2007).

Murphy, Ronald E. *The Tree of Life: An Exploration of the Biblical Wisdom Literature* (Cambridge: Cambridge University Press, 3rd edn, 2002).

Osborne, Grant R. *Revelation,* Baker Exegetical Commentary on the New Testament (Grand Rapids: Baker Academic, 2002).

Prenter, Regin. *Spiritus Creator: Luther's Concept of the Holy Spirit* (trans. John M. Jensen; Philadelphia: Muhlenberg Press, 1953).

Ricoeur, Paul. *Essays on Biblical Interpretation* (ed. Lewis S. Mudge; London: SPCK, 1981).

Sandel, Michael, J. *Justice: What's the Right Thing To Do?* (New York: Farrar, Straus & Giroux, 2009).

Southern, R.W. *The Making of the Middle Ages* (New Haven: Yale University Press, 1961).

Spearing, A.C. *Medieval Dream-Poetry* (Cambridge: Cambridge University Press, 1976).

Swete, Henry Barclay. *The Apocalypse of St John: The Greek text with Introduction, Notes and Indices* (London; New York: Macmillan, 2nd edn, 1907).

Tappert, Theodore G. and others. *The Book of Concord: The Confessions of the Evangelical Lutheran Church* (Philadelphia: Fortress Press, 1959).

Teresa of Avila. *Life: The Complete Works of Saint Teresa of Jesus* (ed. and trans. E. Allison Peers; London: Burns, Oates & Washbourne, 1951).

Teresa, Mother, and Brother Roger. *Meditations on the Way of the Cross* (London: Mowbray, 1986).

The Apostolic Fathers with Justin Martyr and Irenaeus, The Ante-Nicene Fathers: Translations of the Writings of the Fathers down to AD 325, I (ed. Alexander Roberts and James Donaldson, rev. A. Cleveland Coxe; Grand Rapids: Eerdmans, 1985).

—. *St Irenaeus: The Demonstration of the Apostolic Preaching* (trans. J. Robinson; London: SPCK, 1920).

Voaden, R., ed. *Prophets Abroad: The Reception of Continental Holy Women in Late-Medieval England* (Woodbridge: D.S. Brewer, 1996).

Von Balthasar, Hans Urs. *The Glory of the Lord, a Theological Aesthetics: Theology, the Old Covenant*, VI (trans. B. McNeil and E. Leiva-Merikakis, ed. J. Riches; Edinburgh: T&T Clark, 1991).

Ward, Benedicta. *Miracles and the Medieval Mind: Theory, Record and Event 1000–1215* (London: Scolar Press, 1982).

—. *Signs and Wonders: Saints, Miracles and Prayers from the Fourth Century to the Fourteenth Century* (Aldershot: Variorum, 1992).

Watkin-Jones, H. *The Holy Spirit in the Mediaeval Church: A Study of Christian Teaching concerning the Holy Spirit and His Place in the Trinity from the Post-Patristic Age to the Counter-Reformation* (London: The Epworth Press, 1922).

Zizioulas, John D. *Being as Communion* (London: Darton, Longman & Todd, 1985).

Bible Texts

Die Bibel, übersetzt von Franz Eugen Schlachter nach dem hebräischen und griechischen Grundtext (Bielefeld, 2000).

Holy Bible: Containing the Old and New Testaments with the Apocryphal/Deuterocanonical Books, New Revised Standard Version (Oxford: Oxford University Press, 1989).

Novum Testamentum Graece, Nestle-Aland (Stuttgart: Deutsche Bibelgesellschaft, 27th edn, 1993).

Novum Testamentum Latine, Nestle-Aland (Stuttgart: Deutsche Bibelgesellschaft, 1st edn, 1986).

The New Jerusalem Bible (London: Darton, Longman & Todd, reader's edn, 1990).

ENDNOTES

Preface

1 http: www.byfaith.com/paulrevivals.htm (accessed 24 April 2011).

Introduction

1 The idea of returning to the past in order to retrieve lessons to inspire the present (and the future) is encapsulated in the notion of *ressourcement*, a term first used by Charles Péguy (1873–1914) in his description of a people which rebuilds itself 'from an interior movement by a deep return to sources [*ressourcement*] of its ancient pride and by a springing up of the instincts of its race', trans. by Diana Morrison CHN, quoted by Paul Robert in *Le Grand Robert de la Langue Française: Dictionnaire Alphabétique et Analogique de la Langue Française* (rev. Alain Rey; Paris: Le Robert, 2nd edn, 1985), VIII, p. 322.

2 Ronald E. Murphy, *The Tree of Life: An Exploration of the Biblical Wisdom Literature* (Cambridge: CUP, 3rd edn, 2002), p. 59.

3 William James, *The Varieties of Religious Experience: A Study in Human Nature, Being the Gifford Lectures on Natural Religion Delivered at Edinburgh in 1901–1902* (London: Longmans, Green, and Co., 1915), pp. 483–4.

4 David Lewis-Williams, *Conceiving God: The Cognitive Origin and Evolution of Religion* (London: Thomas & Hudson, 2010), hereafter *Conceiving God*, pp. 290–93 (p. 292).

5 Ralf K. Wüstenberg, 'Philosophical Influences on Bonhoeffer's "Religionless Christianity"', in *Bonhoeffer and Continental Thought: Cruciform Philosophy* (ed. Brian Gregor and Jens Zimmermann,

Indiana Series in the Philosophy of Religion (Bloomington: Indiana University Press, 2009), hereafter *Bonhoeffer and Continental Thought*, pp. 137–55 (pp. 143–4).

[6] Bernd Wannenwetsch, 'Introduction: Who is Dietrich Bonhoeffer for Us Today?' in *Who Am I? Bonhoeffer's Theology through His Poetry* (London: T&T Clark, 2009), pp. 1–10 (p. 4).

[7] James Davison Hunter, *To Change the World: The Irony, Tragedy, and Possibility of Christianity in the Late Modern World* (New York: OUP, 2010), p. 185.

1. Crucible of Vision

[1] Hildegard of Bingen, Joseph L. Baird (trans.) and Radd K. Ehrman, eds, *The Letters of Hildegard of Bingen* (3 vols; Oxford: OUP, 1994–2004), hereafter *LHB*, I, 2, pp. 32–3.

[2] 'The Life of Hildegard', in *Jutta and Hildegard: The Biographical Sources* (trans. Anna Silvas; University Park: Pennsylvania State University Press, 1999), hereafter *Jutta and Hildegard*, pp. 135–210 (II, 1, p. 158). 'The Life of Hildegard' is the work by Gottfried of Disibodenberg and Theodoric of Echternach, *Vita Sanctae Hildegardis*, CCCM (ed. Monika Klaes; Turnhout: Brepols, 1993), CXXVI, hereafter *VH*. Theodoric of Echternach is the author of the second and third books completed in the 1180s.

[3] Hildegard of Bingen, *The Book of the Rewards of Life*, Garland Library of Medieval Literature, Series B, vol. 89 (trans. Bruce W. Hozeski; New York; London: Garland, 1994), hereafter *Rewards of Life*, 2, p. 9.

[4] Hildegard of Bingen, 'Life of Hildegard', 1, 1, p. 139.

[5] *Mirrors of the Holy: Ten Studies in Sanctity* (trans. Lucy Menzies; London: A.R. Mowbray, 1928), pp. 5–6, from *Vita*, in *Analecta Sanctae Hildegardis Opera Spicilegio Solesmensi parata* in *Analecta Sacra spicilegio solesmensi* (ed. J.-B. Pitra; Farnborough: *Gregg*, 1966–67), hereafter *Analecta Sanctae Hildegardis*, VIII, p. 332.

[6] 'Eight Readings', in *Jutta and Hildegard*, 2, pp. 211–19 (p. 214).

[7] Guibert, 'Letter to Bovo', in *Jutta and Hildegard*, pp. 99–117 (p. 114).

[8] *LHB* I 40r, 111.

[9] Lewis-Williams, 'Hildegard on the African Veld', in *Conceiving God*, pp. 232–56.

10 Teresa of Avila, *Life: The Complete Works of Saint Teresa of Jesus* (ed. and trans. E. Allison Peers; London: Burns, Oates and Washbourne, 1951), I, XXIX, pp. 192–3.

11 Barbara Newman, 'Hildegard of Bingen: Visions and Validation', *Church History* 54.2 (1985), pp. 163–75 (pp. 167–9); Barbara Newman, 'Three-Part Invention: The *Vita S. Hildegardis* and Mystical Hagiography', in *Hildegard of Bingen: The Context of Her Thought and Art,* Warburg Institute Colloquia, 4 (ed. Charles Burnett and Peter Dronke; London: Warburg Institute, 1998), hereafter *Hildegard*, pp. 189–210 (pp. 198–9).

12 Robert Murray, 'Prophecy in Hildegard', in *Hildegard*, pp. 81–8 (pp. 81–2). The order of the tests has been inverted to facilitate the flow of the argument.

13 *Rewards of Life*, 2, p. 9, *LHB* I, 23, p. 76; I, 1, p. 27.

14 Hildegard of Bingen, 'Life of Hildegard', 1, 8, p. 150.

15 See, for example, *Hildegard Bingensis Liber Vite Meritorum*, CCCM (ed. Angela Carlevaris; Turnhout: Brepols, 1995), XC, hereafter *LVM* = *Rewards of Life*, I, 83.1446, 91.1558, 94.1596, 121.1864; II, 61.1263, 68.1375, 76.1504, 79.1540; III, 46.1111, 50.1174, 54.1223, 57.1263, 64.1360, 71.1453; see, for example, *LVM* I, 76.1341, 87.1500, 105.1717; II, 57.1195, 64.1308, 71.1437, 82.1570.

16 Hildegard of Bingen, *Hildegard Bingensis LiberDiuinorum Operum,* CCCM (ed. A. Derolez and P. Dronke; Turnhout: Brepols, 1996), XCII, hereafter *LDO* = *Divine Works*, Introduction, pp. lxxxiii–iv, 'Epilogus', pp. 463–4. The miniatures that are referred to are those in the thirteenth-century codex at Lucca.

17 *LHB* I, 1r, p. 31.

18 Trans. from *VH* II, 2.96–7, p. 24.

19 Beverly Mayne Kienzle, *Hildegard of Bingen and Her Gospel Homilies: Speaking New Mysteries,* Medieval Women: Texts and Contexts, vol. 12 (Brepols: Turnhout, 2009), hereafter *Homilies*, p. 37; Newman, 'Visions and Validations', 163–75 (p. 22); Constant J. Mews, 'Hildegard, Visions and Religious Reform', in *'Im Angesicht Gottes suche der Menschen sich selbst': Hildegard von Bingen (1098–1179)*, Erudiri Sapientia, II (ed. Rainer Berndt; Berlin, Akademie Verlag, 2003), hereafter *Angesicht Gottes*, pp. 325–42 (p. 341).

20 Murray, *Hildegard*, p. 87.

21 John of Salisbury, *Policraticus* (ed. Clement C.J. Webb; Oxford: 1909), I, 2, 29, p. 166; trans. by Benedicta Ward in *Miracles and the Medieval*

Mind: Theory, Record and Event 1000–1215 (London: Scolar Press, 1982), p. 12. *Hildegard of Bingen: Selected Writings* (trans. Mark Atherton; London: Penguin, 2001), pp. xviii–xix, quotes *The Letters of John of Salisbury: The Later Letters (1163–80)* (ed. and trans. W.J. Millor and C.L.N. Brooke; Oxford, 1979), II, 185, p. 224.

22 Theodoric of Echternach (trans. Silvas), II, 4, pp. 162–3.

23 Mews, in *'Angesicht Gottes'*, p. 325.

24 Hildegard of Bingen, *Symphonia Armonie Celestium Revelationum* (ed. and trans. Barbara Newman; Ithaca, NY; London: Cornell University Press, 2nd edn, 1998), hereafter *SYM*, 8, v. 5a, p. 151. Newman's poetic interpretations have been used rather than her literal translations.

25 Trans. from *Guiberti Gemblacensis Epistolae,* Part 1, Epistolae I–XXIV, CCCM (ed. Albert Derolez; Turnhout: Brepols, 1988), LXVI, 18.242– 53, p. 232.

26 *LHB* I, n. 1, p. 98; I, 40, p. 110.

27 Kienzle, *Gospel Homilies*, p. 51. Beverly Mayne Kienzle, 'Constructing Heaven in Hildegard of Bingen's *Expositiones euangeliorum'*, in *Envisaging Heaven in the Middle Ages*, Routledge Studies in Medieval Religion and Culture (ed. Carolyn Muessig and Ad Putter; Oxford: Routledge, 2007), pp. 34–43 (p. 34); Beverly Mayne Kienzle, *Cistercians, Heresy and Crusade in Occitania, 1145–1229: Preaching in the Lord's Vineyard* (Woodbridge: York Medieval Press, 2001), hereafter *Cistercians*, p. 4; Newman, in *Hildegard*, pp. 204–5.

28 II, 1, p. 155.

29 Quoted by Florence Eliza Glaze, 'Medical Writer: "Behold the Human Creature"', in *Voice of the Living Light: Hildegard of Bingen and Her World* (ed. Barbara Newman; Berkeley, CA; London: University of California Press, 1998), hereafter *Voice*, pp. 125–48 (p. 125).

30 Peter Dronke, *Women Writers of the Middle Ages: A Critical Study of Texts from Perpetua (+203) to Marguerite Porete (+1310)* (Cambridge, CUP, 1984), hereafter *Women Writers*, pp. 144–210 (p. 144).

31 Gunilla Iversen, '"O vos angeli": Hildegard's Lyrical and Visionary Texts on the Celestial Hierarchies in the Context of Her Time', in *'Angesicht Gottes'*, pp. 87-113 (p. 112). Barbara Newman, 'Poet: "Where the Living Majesty Utters Mysteries"', in *Voice*, pp. 178–92 (p. 181); Menzies, p. 4; Peter Dronke, *Poetic Individuality in the Middle Ages: New Departures in Poetry 1000–1150* (Oxford: Clarendon Press, 1970), pp. 157–8.

32 Trans. in Introduction, p. xxxviii, *LDO* I, 1, 2.5–7, p. 48; http://real-doctorjay.com/quotes-hildegard-bingen/ (accessed 22 November 2010); *LHB* I, 15r, p. 55, cf. *LHB*, I, 77r, pp. 166–71.

33 http://www.imdb.com/title/tt0995850/fullcredits (accessed 29 November 2010).

34 Elizabeth A. Dreyer, *Passionate Spirituality: Hildegard of Bingen and Hadewijch of Brabant* (New York: Paulist Press, 2005), pp. 98–101.

35 Brian Gregor, 'Bonhoeffer's "Christian Social Philosophy": Conscience, Alterity, and the Moment of Ethical Responsibility', in *Bonhoeffer and Continental Thought*, pp. 201–25 (pp. 206–14).

36 Quoted by Eberhard Bethge, *Dietrich Bonhoeffer: Theologian, Christian, Man for His Times* (rev. and ed. Victoria J. Barnett; Minneapolis: Fortress Press, 2000), hereafter *Bonhoeffer*, p. 867.

37 Dietrich Bonhoeffer, *Spiritual Care* (trans. Jay C. Rochelle; Philadelphia: Fortress Press, 1985), p. 49 ('Seelsorge', *Gesammelte Schriften* (5 vols; Munich: C. Kaiser, 1965–72), hereafter *GS*, V, pp. 384–5).

38 Bethge, *Bonhoeffer*, pp. 204–5.

39 See Regin Prenter, *Spiritus Creator: Luther's Concept of the Holy Spirit* (trans. John M. Jensen; Philadelphia: Muhlenberg Press, 1953), hereafter *Spiritus Creator*, pp. 55, 64.

40 Dietrich Bonhoeffer, *Act and Being* (ed. Wayne Whitson Floyd Jr., trans. H. Martin Rumscheidt; Minneapolis: Fortress Press, 1996), hereafter *AB*, pp. 55–9.

41 Karl Barth, *The Word of God and the Word of Man* (trans. Douglas Horton; London, Hodder & Stoughton, 1928), p. 83, cf. pp. 287–8.

42 Karl Barth, *The Epistle to the Romans* (trans. from the 6th edn by Edwyn H. Hoskyns; London: H. Milford, 1933), p. 112.

43 Bonhoeffer, 'The Theology of Crisis and Its Attitude toward Philosophy and Science', 1931, in *GS* III, pp. 110–26 (p. 111). References in this section are to this lecture, pp. 111–14, 123.

44 *GS* V, p. 307.

45 *GS* I, p. 358.

46 Trans. from *GS* I, p. 64.

47 Trans. from *GS* III, p. 56.

48 Trans. from *GS* I, p. 34.

49 *GS* IV, p. 55.

50 *GS* IV, p. 180.

[51] Trans. from 'Die Geschichte der systematischen Theologie des 20. Jahrhunderts', Berlin Lecture, 1931/33, *GS* V, pp. 181–227 (p. 216), hereafter 'Die Geschichte'.

[52] Gerhard Ebeling, *Word and Faith* (trans. J.C.B. Mohr; London: SCM, 1963), p. 285 (*GS* II, p. 63).

[53] *GS* I, pp. 230–39.

[54] *Discipleship* (ed. Geffrey B. Kelly and John D. Godsey, trans. Barbara Green and Reinhard Krauss; Minneapolis: Fortress Press, 2001), hereafter *D* p. 81.

[55] See *D* pp. 225–52.

[56] *D* p. 232.

[57] *D* p. 233.

[58] Dietrich Bonhoeffer, *The Way to Freedom: Letters, Lectures and Notes 1935-1939 from the Collected Works of Dietrich Bonhoeffer*, II (trans. Edwin H. Robertson and John Bowden; London: Collins, 1966), hereafter *WF*, pp. 93–4 (*GS* II, pp. 238–9).

[59] 'Zur Frage nach der Kirchengemeinschaft', 21 April 1936, *GS* IV, pp. 217–41.

[60] Trans. from 'Der Wiederaufbau Jerusalems nach Esra und Nehemia', *GS* IV, p. 335.

[61] Dietrich Bonhoeffer, *No Rusty Swords: Letters, Lectures and Notes 1928–1936 from the Collected Works of Dietrich Bonhoeffer*, I (trans. Edwin H. Robertson and John Bowden; London: Collins, 1965), hereafter *NRS* p. 117 (*GS* II, p. 285).

[62] Trans. by Ebeling, p. 283 (*GS* I, p. 42).

[63] *WF* pp. 70–71 (*GS* II, pp. 499–500).

[64] *WF* p. 130 (*GS* I, p. 269).

[65] Dietrich Bonhoeffer, *Life Together and Prayerbook of the Bible* (ed. Geffrey B. Kelly, trans. Daniel W. Bloesch and James H. Burtness; Minneapolis: Fortress Press, 1996), hereafter *LT*, p. 51.

[66] Susan Quaintance, 'Dietrich Bonhoeffer and Benedictine Monasticism: *Life Together'*, *The American Benedictine Review* 48 (1997): pp. 347–60 (p. 356). See *The Rule of St Benedict in English* (ed. Timothy Fry; Collegeville: The Liturgical Press, 1982), hereafter *Rule*.

[67] 'Prologue', 50, in *Rule*, pp. 18–19.

[68] *LT* p. 34.

[69] 'Prologue', 1, in *Rule*, p. 15.

[70] *LT* p. 84.

[71] Thomas à Kempis, *The Imitation of Christ* (rev. Harold J. Chadwick; Nashville: Bridge-Logos, 1999), hereafter *Imitation*.

[72] À Kempis, *Imitation*, I, 20, p. 21, I, cf. III, 8, pp. 64–5, cf. *LT* p. 81.

[73] À Kempis, *Imitation*, I, 20, p. 20. LT p. 85.

[74] *LT* p. 89.

[75] À Kempis, *Imitation*, II, 9, p. 45, cf. II, 9, pp. 48–50, II, 9, pp 50–54.

[76] *LT* p. 98.

[77] À Kempis, *Imitation*, II, 2, p. 38, cf. *LT* p. 96.

[78] *AB* p. 85, n. 8, cf. *AB* pp. 90–91.

[79] Dietrich Bonhoeffer, *Ethics* (ed. Clifford J. Green, trans. Reinhard Krauss, Charles C. West and Douglas W. Stott; Minneapolis: Fortress Press, 2005), hereafter *E*, pp. 43–5.

[80] Trans. from *GS* v, p. 226.

[81] *E* p. 403.

[82] Theodoric of Echternach (trans. Silvas), 'Life of Hildegard', 2.6, p. 167.

2. Scripture and Vision

[1] Proper 28, Preface of the Lord's Day, in *The Book of Common Prayer and Administration of the Sacraments and Other Rites and Ceremonies of the Church together with the Psalter and Psalms of David, according to the Use of the Episcopal Church* (New York: The Church Hymnal Corporation, 1979).

[2] Brevard S. Childs, 'On Reclaiming the Bible for Christian Theology', in *Reclaiming the Bible for the Church* (ed. Carl E. Braaten and Robert W. Jensen; Edinburgh: T&T Clark, 1995), pp. 1–17 (pp. 7–8), hereafter *Reclaiming the Bible*, Hans Urs Von Balthasar, *The Glory of the Lord, a Theological Aesthetics: Theology, the Old Covenant* (trans. B. McNeil and E. Leiva-Merikakis, ed. J. Riches; Edinburgh: T&T Clark, 1991), vi, pp. 402–4, A.G. Herbert, *The Throne of David: A Study of the Fulfilment of the Old Testament in Jesus Christ and His Church* (London: Faber & Faber, 1941), pp. 33–8, Walter Brueggemann, *Theology of the Old Testament: Testimony, Dispute, Advocacy* (Minneapolis: Fortress, 1997).

[3] Andrew Louth, *Discerning the Mystery: An Essay on the Nature of Theology* (Oxford: Clarendon Press, 1983), pp. 103–5, Paul Ricoeur, *Essays on Biblical Interpretation* (ed. Lewis S. Mudge; London: SPCK,

1981), pp. 50–57, Brevard S. Childs, 'Toward Recovering Theological Exegesis', *Ex Auditu* 16 (2000): pp. 121–9, hereafter referred to as 'Theological Exegesis', p. 122.

4 Henri de Lubac, *Medieval Exegesis: The Four Senses of Scripture* (2 vols, trans. Mark Sebanc; Edinburgh: T&T Clark 1998–2000), hereafter *Exegesis*, I, pp. 232–3.

5 Henri de Lubac, *Catholicism: A Study of Dogma in Relation to the Corporate Destiny of Mankind* (trans. Lancelot C. Sheppard; London: Burns, Oates & Washbourne, 1950), hereafter *Catholicism*, p. 85.

6 *Catholicism*, p. 91.

7 G.R. Evans, T*he Thought of Gregory the Great* (Cambridge: CUP, 1986), p. 148, trans. from Guibert of Nogent, *Guiberti Opera Omnia: Moralia in Genesim* (Paris, 1853), PL, CLVI, col. 314C.

8 Jean Leclercq, *The Love of Learning and the Desire for God: A Study of Monastic Culture* (trans. C. Misrahi; New York: Fordham University Press, 1974), p. 290.

9 Hildegard of Bingen, *Scivias*, Classics of Western Spirituality (ed. and trans. Columba Hart and Jane Bishop; New York: Paulist Press, 1990), III, 13, 13, hereafter *Scivias*, p. 533.

10 Hildegard of Bingen, *Hildegard of Bingen's Book of Divine Works, with Letters and Songs* (ed. Matthew Fox, trans. Robert Cunningham; Sante Fe, NM: Bear & Co., 1987), hereafter *Divine Works*, III, 10, 20, p. 245.

11 C.S. Lewis, *The Allegory of Love: A Study in Medieval Tradition* (Oxford: OUP, 1958), pp. 113, 44–8.

12 *LHB* II, pp. 23-4.

13 Trans. from *LVM* II, 1.6–16, p. 72. For interpretation of vision see *Rewards of Life*, II, 20.29 – 24.33, pp. 82–4.

14 *SYM* 65, v. 5, p. 245.

15 *LHB* III, 'Meditation', 374, p. 161.

16 *LHB* III, 'Songs and Meditations, 1173–79', 390, p. 199.

17 Hildegard of Bingen, *Hildegard Bingensis Scivias*, CCCM (ed. Adelgundis Führkötter and Angela Carlevaris; Turnhout: Brepols 1978), XLIII-XLIIIA, hereafter *SC*, II, 2, 7.156–60, trans. Mark Atherton, *Hildegard of Bingen: Selected Writings* (London: Penguin, 2001), p. 27. *SC* = *Scivias*.

18 Trans. from *LDO* I, 4, 105.96–97, p. 251.

19 *LHB* I, p. 55.

20 *LHB* I, p. 171.

21 *LHB* III, 162, n. 2, cf. III, pp. 19, 23, n. 2.

22 *LHB* I, 23, p. 79.

23 Trans. from *LDO* II, 1, 13.8–10, p. 280.

24 De Lubac, *Exegesis* I, p. 79, Augustine, *In ps.* 8, n. 7–9.

25 Gregory the Great, *The Author Is the Holy Spirit: The Commentary on Job*, in *Early Medieval Theology*, The Library of Christian Classics (ed. and trans. G.E. McCracken and A. Cabaniss; London: SCM, 1957), Preface, II, 9, p. 190.

26 *John Cassian: The Conferences,* Ancient Christian Writers, The Works of the Fathers in Translation (trans. Boniface Ramsey, LVII; New York: Paulist Press, 1997), I, 10, 11.4, p. 384.

27 The notes in this paragraph are taken from Kienzle, *Homilies*, 2009, pp. 43, 79, 163–7, *Expositiones Euangeliorum* (ed. Beverly Kienzle and Carolyn A. Muessig), in *Hildergardis Bingensis Opera Minora*, CCCM, 226 (ed. Peter Dronke, Christopher P. Evans, Hugh Feiss, Beverly Mayne Kienzle, Carolyn A. Muessig, and Barbara Newman; Turnhout: Brepols, 2007), pp. 185–333 (46-8, pp. 311-15); see also Kienzle, *Cistercians*, pp. 74–5.

28 *Rewards of Life*, II, 30.39, p. 87.

29 *SYM*, 'Antiphon for Patriarchs and Prophets', 31.1–9, pp. 158–9.

30 *SYM*, 'Responsory for Patriarchs and Prophets', 32.1–6, p. 161.

31 *Scivias* I, 3.1, p. 94.

32 *LHB* I, 3, p. 34.

33 *LHB* I, 23, pp. 76–9.

34 Cited by Alister E. McGrath, 'Reclaiming our Roots and Vision', in *Reclaiming the Bible*, p. 67.

35 Trans. from *GS* III, p. 299.

36 *The Young Bonhoeffer, 1918–1927* (ed. Paul Duane Matheny, Clifford J. Green and Marshall D. Johnson, trans. Mary C. Nebelsick assisted by Douglas W. Stott; Minneapolis: Fortress Press, 2003), hereafter *YB*, p. 296.

37 *Creation and Fall* (ed. John W. de Gruchy, trans. Douglas Stephen Bax; Minneapolis: Fortress Press, 1997), hereafter *CF*, pp. 22–3, 83.

38 'Vergegenwärtigung neutestamentlicher Texte', Hauteroda, *GS* III, pp. 303–24 (pp. 305–20). All references in the following section are from this lecture.

39 Trans. of Bethge's comment in 'Dietrich Bonhoeffer und die Juden', *Konsequenzen: Dietrich Bonhoeffers Kirchenverständnis heute,* Internationales Bonhoeffer Forum, Forschung und Praxis, 3 (ed. Ernst Feil and Ilse Tödt; Munich: Kaiser, 1980), p. 182.

[40] 'König David', three Bible studies with the brotherhood of the Pomeranian curates, 8–11 October 1935, Finkenwalde, *GS* IV, pp. 294–320 (p. 320). All references in the following section are translations from these studies.

[41] Bethge, in 'Dietrich Bonhoeffer und die Juden', p. 182, cf. *GS* II, p. 292.

[42] 'Christus in den Psalmen', lecture for the Pomeranian students of the Confessing Church, 31 July 1935, Finkenwalde, *GS* III, pp. 295–300. All references in the following section are translations from this lecture.

[43] 'Meditation über Psalm 58', 11 July 1937, Finkenwalde, *GS* IV, pp. 413–22 (*GS* IV, pp. 422–26). See *Meditating on the Word* (trans. and ed. David McI. Gracie; Cambridge, MA: Cowley, 1986), hereafter *MW*, pp. 85–96.

[44] *Expositions on the Book of Psalms by Saint Augustin Bishop of Hippo*, A Select Library of the Nicene and Post-Nicene Fathers of the Christian Church, VIII (ed. A. Cleveland Coxe; Grand Rapids: Eerdmans, 1974), p. 563.

[45] *Life Together and Prayerbook of the Bible* (ed. Geffrey B. Kelly, trans. Daniel W. Bloesch and James H. Burtness; Minneapolis: Fortress Press, 1996), hereafter *PB*, p. 164.

[46] *PB* p. 170.

[47] *LT* p. 63.

[48] *LT* p. 12.

[49] *PB* p. 159.

[50] *PB* p. 160.

[51] *LT* p. 57.

[52] *PB* p. 161.

[53] *PB* p. 161, Luther, 'Auslegung des 67 Psalms' (n. p. 1521), 39, 220.

[54] *LT* p. 87.

[55] *MW* pp. 43–4.

[56] Bethge, *Bonhoeffer*, p. 511.

[57] *WF* p. 233 (*GS* I, pp. 303–4).

[58] Cf. Bethge, *Bonhoeffer*, p. 655.

[59] *Letters and Papers from Prison* (ed. Eberhard Bethge; London: SCM, enlarged edn, 1971), hereafter *LPP*, p. 27.

3. Community of Vision

[1] De Lubac, *Catholicism*, pp. 177–92, see Appendix, pp. 208–83.

[2] Henri de Lubac, *The Drama of Atheist Humanism* (trans. Edith M. Riley; London: Sheed & Ward, 1949), pp. v, 6–17, hereafter *Humanism*.

3 Henri de Lubac, *The Discovery of God* (trans. Alexander Dru, notes trans. Mark Sebanc and Cassian Fulcom (Edinburgh: T&T Clark, 1960), p. 7.

4 Henri de Lubac, *The Mystery of the Supernatural* (trans. Rosemary Sheed; London: G. Chapman, 1967), hereafter *Supernatural*, pp. 27, 109, 97–130.

5 Irenaeus, 'Irenaeus against Heresies', *The Apostolic Fathers with Justin Martyr and Irenaeus*, I, The Ante-Nicene Fathers: Translations of the Writings of the Fathers down to AD 325 (ed. Alexander Roberts and James Donaldson, rev. A. Cleveland Coxe; Grand Rapids: Eerdmans, 1985), IV, Preface, 4, p. 463; IV, 20, 1, pp. 487-8. Further references to Irenaeus in this chapter are to this work.

6 V, 5, 1, p. 531.

7 V, 5, 2, p. 531.

8 V, 15, 2, p. 543, cf. V, 1, 3, p. 527, for the metaphor of the hand as a link between the creation and recreation of Adam.

9 Justin Martyr, 'Justin's Apology on Behalf of Christians', in *Justin, Philosopher and Martyr: Apologies* (ed. with commentary on the text, Denis Minns and Paul Parvis; Oxford: OUP, 2009), 36.1, p. 179.

10 Henry Barclay Swete, *The Apocalypse of St John: The Greek Text with Introduction, Notes and Indices* (London: Macmillan, 2nd edn, 1907), p. 249; Grant R. Osborne, Revelation, Baker Exegetical Commentary on the New Testament (Grand Rapids: Baker Academic, 2002), p. 678; for a summary of the interpretative tradition of this phrase, see pp. 677–8.

11 Austin Farrer, *The Glass of Vision*, Bampton Lectures, 1948 (Westminster: Dacre, 1948), pp. 128, 130.

12 Peter Dronke, 'Hildegard's Inventions', in *Hildegard von Bingenin ihrem wissenschaftlicher Kongreß zum 900 jährigen Jubiläum, 13–19. September 1998, Bingen am Rhein* (ed. Alfred Haverkamp; Mainz: Verlag Phillip von Zabern, 2000), p. 314, in William Harmless SJ, *Mystics* (New York: OUP, 2008), pp. 70–72.

13 R.W. Southern, *The Making of the Middle Ages* (New Haven: Yale University Press, 1961), p. 226.

14 *Divine Works*, 4, 12, p. 87.

15 *SYM* 54, pp. 213, 215.

16 *SYM* 35.1, p. 167, *SYM* 28, v. 2b, p. 149.

17 Gerard Manley Hopkins, extract from unfinished poems and fragments 1876–89, 'Margaret Clitheroe', *Poems and Prose of Gerard Manley*

Hopkins (ed. W. H. Gardner; Harmondsworth: Penguin, 1953), 58, p. 78.

[18] H. Watkin-Jones, *The Holy Spirit in the Mediaeval Church: A Study of Christian Teaching concerning the Holy Spirit and His Place in the Trinity from the Post-Patristic Age to the Counter-Reformation* (London: The Epworth Press, 1922), pp. 332, 323.

[19] Augustine of Hippo, *The Trinity*, The Fathers of the Church: A New Translation, XLV (trans. Stephen McKenna; Washington, The Catholic University of America Press, 1963), hereafter *Trinity*, IV, 21, p. 170.

[20] *Scivias*, II, 2, 2, pp. 161–2.

[21] Trans. from *LDO*, I, 1.2.42, p. 49.

[22] Trans. from Augustine, *De Doctrina Christiana* (Paris, 1841), PL, XXXIV, I.5.5.

[23] *LHB* I, 31r, pp. 95–7, see Hildegard of Bingen, *Hildegard Bingensis Epistolarium*, CCCM (ed. Lieven van Acker, XCI–XCIA, ed. Lieven van Acker and Monika Klaes-Hachmöller, XCIB; Turnhout: Brepols, 1991-2001), hereafter *EP*, XCI, 31r.12–21, 66–73, 100–10, pp. 83–6. References in the following analysis are to these sources.

[24] Hildegard, *Hildegard of Bingen: On Natural Philosophy and Medicine* (ed. and trans. Margaret Berger; Cambridge: D.S. Brewer, 1999), hereafter *Natural Philosophy*, pp. 23–4.

[25] Trans. from 'Opuscula: "Liber compositae medicinae de aegritudinum causis, signis atque curis, *De Mundi Creatione* I,"' in *Analecta Sanctae Hildegardis*, VIII, p. 469.

[26] *Divine Works*, I, 2, 1.1–48, pp. 59–61.

[27] *Scivias*, II, 5, 32, p. 220.

[28] *Scivias*, III, 13, 7, p. 528.

[29] *SYM*, 'Antiphon for Patriarchs and Prophets', 31.14–15, p. 159.

[30] *LHB* III, 'Songs and Meditations, before 1173', 390, p. 193.

[31] I, 4, 100.2, p. 243; VI, 32.709–10, p. 286.

[32] *LHB* III, 'Prayers and Meditations about Prophecy, 1173–79', 389, p. 191.

[33] *LHB* III, 'Songs and Meditations, before 1173', 390, p. 198.

[34] *Rewards of Life*, I, 15.27, p. 17.

[35] *Scivias* II, 2, p. 161.

[36] Trans. from *SC* II.2, 2.31–2, p. 125, cf. Charleton T. Lewis and Charles Short, *A Latin Dictionary* (Oxford: Clarendon Press, 1st edn, 1879).

[37] Trans. from *LVM* II, 52.1084, p. 103; Benedicta Ward, *Signs and Wonders: Saints, Miracles and Prayers from the Fourth Century to the Fourteenth Century* (Aldershot: Variorum, 1992), p. 105.

38 *Scivias* III, 8, 19, p. 442.

39 *SC* II, 1.77–84, p. 111, trans. Atherton, p. 10.

40 *Scivias* II, 3, p. 169, with the explanation of the vision in II, 3, 14, p. 174.

41 *LHB* II, 149r, p. 92.

42 Trans. from *Expositio Evangeliorum: In Nativitate Domini, Ad Primam Missam*, in *Analecta Sanctae Hildegardis*, VIII, II, I, p. 247.

43 Hildegard, *Causae et Curae* (trans. Berger), in *Natural Philosophy*, I, 14a, b, p. 34.

44 *Divine Works*, I, 16, p. 74.

45 *LDO* III, 3, 2.28–30, p. 380, trans. in Introduction, p. lxxiii.

46 *LHB* I, 39r, p. 109.

47 *Scivias* II, 2, 6, p. 164.

48 *Rewards of Life*, IV, 36.47, p. 197.

49 *LDO*, Introduction, p. Xxxii, see I, 3, 3.24, p. 121, I, 3, 4.6–7, p. 121.

50 Hildegard of Bingen, Finale, *Ordo Virtutum*, in *Nine Medieval Latin Plays* (ed. and trans. Peter Dronke; Cambridge: CUP, 1994), lines 255, 258–66, p. 181.

51 *Ordo Virtutum* (trans. Dronke), lines 267–9, p. 181.

52 *Scivias* III, 12, p. 515.

53 *SYM*, 'Hymn to Saint Ursula', 65, p. 245.

54 Dietrich Bonhoeffer, *Lectures on Christology* (trans. Edwin Robertson; London: Collins, 1978), pp. 45–6.

55 See Joel Lawrence, *Bonhoeffer: A Guide for the Perplexed* (London: T&T Clark International, 2010), pp. 11–53. See also, G.A. Studdert Kennedy, *The Unutterable Beauty* (London: Hodder & Stoughton, 1941), pp. 34–5.

56 Martin Luther, LW, XXII, *Sermons on the Gospel of St John: Chapters 1 – 4* (ed. Jaroslav Pelikan; St Louis: Concordia Publishing House, 1957), I, pp. 9–10, 13.

57 Alister E. McGrath, *Luther's Theology of the Cross: Martin Luther's Theological Breakthrough* (Oxford: Blackwell, 1985), pp. 149–51, Regin Prenter, 'Bonhoeffer and the Young Luther', in *World Come of Age: A Symposium on Dietrich Bonhoeffer* (ed. Ronald Gregor Smith; London: Collins, 1967), pp. 161–81 (p. 162), trans. from *Unbekannte Fragmente aus Luthers zweiter Psalmenvorlesung*, 1518 (ed. Erich Vogelsang; Berlin, 1940), pp. 8–28.

58 *D* p. 283, see *Cassell's German and English Dictionary* (rev. Harold T. Betteridge; London: Cassells, 12th edn, 1976), Rose Nash, *Multilingual*

Lexicon of Linguistics and Philology: English, Russian, German and French, Miami Linguistics Series No 3 (Florida, 1968), pp. 40, 78, 83–4.

59 *D* pp. 214, 283–4.

60 *D* pp. 284–7.

61 *D* pp. 226–8.

62 *E* pp. 97–9; Clifford J. Green, *Bonhoeffer: A Theology of Sociality* (Grand Rapids: Eerdmans, 1999), p. 120.

63 *D* p. 63, *Solida Declaratio* III, 'The Righteousness of Faith before God', in *The Book of Concord, the Confessions of the Evangelical Lutheran Church* (ed. and trans. Theodore G. Tappert and others; Philadelphia: Fortress, 1959), p. 540, *LPP* p. 286.

64 *E* pp. 231, 257.

65 Dietrich Bonhoeffer, *Sanctorum Communio* (ed. Clifford J. Green, trans. Reinhard Krauss and Nancy Lukens; Minneapolis: Fortress, 1998), hereafter *SC*, pp. 120, 146, 155, cf. pp. 122, 155, 156, 184; see also *AB* p. 87, n. 14, p. 120, *E* p. 288.

66 *D* pp. 90, 191, 217, 222.

67 *SC* p. 243, *D* p. 140.

68 *LT* pp. 101–2, 109.

69 *E* pp. 257–9.

70 Trans. from 'Sonntag nach Trinitatis', 12 June 1932, Col. 3:1–4, *GS* IV, p. 77; Bonhoeffer, quoted by Geffrey B. Kelly and F. Burton Nelson in *The Cost of Moral Leadership: The Spirituality of Dietrich Bonhoeffer* (Grand Rapids, Cambridge: Eerdmans, 2003), hereafter *Moral Leadership*, pp. 6–7, 175; *LPP* pp. 369–70; Mother Teresa and Brother Roger, *Meditations on the Way of the Cross* (London: Mowbray, 1986), p. 54.

71 *LPP* pp. 337, 360, 370.

72 Trans. by Kelly, in Bethge, *Bonhoeffer*, p. 830.

73 *SC* pp. 118–21.

74 *SC* p. 140.

75 Trans. from 'Das Predigtwort', in 'Finkenwalder Homiletik', p. 240.

76 John D. Zizioulas, *Being as Communion* (London: Darton, Longman & Todd, 1985), p. 15.

77 De Lubac, *Humanism*, pp. 6–17.

78 Ludwig Feuerbach, *Lectures on the Essence of Religion* (trans. Ralph Manheim; New York: Harper & Row, 1967), pp. 177, 188.

79 Feuerbach (trans. Manheim), *Essence*, p. 285.

80 Feuerbach, 'Preface of 1843', in *The Essence of Christianity* (trans. George Eliot; New York: Harper & Brothers Publishers, 1957), pp. xxxvi–xxxvii.

81 'Die Geschichte', *GS* v, p. 187.
82 *AB* p. 115.
83 *LPP* p. 355.
84 *LPP* pp. 348–9.
85 *LPP* pp. 33, 35.

4. Visionary Dreamers

1 Irenaeus, 'Rule of Faith', in *St Irenaeus: The Demonstration of the Apostolic Preaching* (trans. J. Robinson; London: SPCK, 1920), V, p. 36.
2 John Milbank, *The Suspended Middle: Henri de Lubac and the Debate concerning the Supernatural* (Grand Rapids: Eerdmans, 2005), p. 64.
3 *Catholicism*, p. 178.
4 *Supernatural*, pp. xi–xii, 48, 70–72.
5 Eric Lee, 'From Copenhagen to Cambrai: Paradoxes of Faith in Kierkegaard and de Lubac', in *Belief and Metaphysics* (ed. Conor Cunningham and Peter M. Candler; London: SCM, 2007), pp. 252–4.
6 Cf. J.N.D. Kelly, *A Commentary on the Epistles of Peter and of Jude* (London: A&C Black, 1969), p. 323, Jonathan Knight, *2 Peter and Jude*, New Testament Guides (Sheffield: Sheffield Academic Press, 1995), p. 62.
7 Cf. Kelly, p. 324.
8 Augustine (trans. McKenna), in *Trinity*, 9, 1 (1), p. 270; 1, 6 (13), p. 17.
9 Augustine (trans. McKenna), in *Trinity*, 5, 11 (12), pp. 189–90.
10 Watkin-Jones, pp. 331–52.
11 Theodoric of Echternach (trans. Silvas), 'Life of Hildegard', II, 3, pp. 160–61.
12 Trans. from Rupert of Deutz, *Opera Omnia, De Glorificatione Trinitatis et Processione Sancti Spiritus* (Paris, 1854), PL, CLXIX, I, XI, 11 col. 23.
13 Divine Works, I, 2, p. 11.
14 *Divine Works*, III, 4, p. 64.
15 *LDO* III, 2, 14.77–8, p. 375, trans. in Introduction, p. lxxii.
16 Trans. from *LVM* II, 2, 52.1083–7, p. 103.
17 *Rewards of Life*, II, 2, 30.39, p. 87; text in brackets is my translation.
18 *Divine Works*, III, 15, p. 74.
19 Trans. from *LVM* IV, 14.290–91, 293, p. 181.
20 *LHB* I, 15r, Appendix II, p. 63.
21 *LHB* I, 41, p. 113.

22 *LHB* I, 18r, p. 70.

23 'Chants for the Trinity: Holy Spirit', in *Symphonia Armonie Celestium Revelationum* (8 vols, ed. and trans. Marianne Richert Pfau; Bryn Mawr, PA: Hildegard Publishing Co., 1997), VIII.

24 *SYM*, 'Antiphon for the Holy Spirit', 24, p. 141.6–7.

25 *SYM*, 'Hymn to the Holy Spirit', 27, p. 147.

26 Pfau, 'Sequence for the Holy Spirit', 28, vv. 1b, 2a.

27 *SYM*, 'Hymn to the Holy Spirit', 27, v. 4, p. 145.

28 V. 5, p. 145.

29 V. 9, p. 145.

30 33.7–8, p. 163.

31 See, for example, Matthew 3:11; Mark 3:29; 13:11; Luke 10:21; John 14:16,17,26; 15:26; 16:7–15; 17; Acts 5:3; 7:51; 9:31; 15:28; 20:23; 21:11; 28:25.

32 See Newman, *SYM* p. 57; Peter Van Poucke, *Symphonia Harmoniae Caelestium Revelationum*, facsimile ed. of Dendermonde ms with music (Peer: Alamire, 1991).

33 *The Prayers and Meditations of St Anselm* (trans. Benedicta Ward; Harmondsworth: Penguin, 1973), pp. 110–14 (p. 112.87–9).

34 *SYM*, 'Antiphon for the Virgin', 15.5–8, p. 121.

35 Anselm (trans. Ward), p. 113.107–8.

36 *SYM*, 'Antiphon for the Virgin', 14.4–7, p. 119.

37 *SYM*, 'Responsory for the Virgin', 9, p. 113.

38 See S.F. Kruger, *Dreaming in the Middle Ages* (Cambridge: CUP, 1992).

39 *Bede: Ecclesiastical History of the English People, with Bede's Letter to Egberg and Cuthbert's Letter on the Death of Bede* (trans. Leo Sherley-Price; London: Penguin Books, rev. edn, 1990), V, 12, pp. 285–8.

40 A.C. Spearing, *Medieval Dream-Poetry* (Cambridge: CUP, 1976), pp. 9–10, from *Commentary on the Dream of Scipio* (trans. W.H. Stahl; New York, 1952), pp. 88, 90.

41 John of Salisbury, *Frivolities of Courtiers and Footprints of Philosophers: A Translation of Books I, II, III and Selections from Books VII and VIII of the Policraticus* (trans. Joseph B. Pike; London, H. Milford: 1938), II, 89, pp. 77, 94, 81.

42 Trans. from *VH* II, 9.17–24, p. 33.

43 *LHB*, 103r II, p. 24.

44 Trans. from *LDO* III, 2, 10.54–6, p. 368.

45 Trans. from *VH* II, 11.38–40, p. 36.

46 Trans. from *LVM* I, 17, 356–60, pp. 20–21.

47 Trans. from *EP* xci, 1.48–9, p. 5.
48 Trans. from *LDO* I, 5 (6).9–11, p. 52.
49 Dietrich Bonhoeffer, 'Paper on the Historical and Pneumatological Interpretation of Scripture' (1925), in *YB* pp. 285–98, p. 293.
50 *YB*, 'Luther's Views of the Holy Spirit according to the Disputationem of 1535–1545 edited by Drews' (1926), pp. 325–70.
51 *YB* pp. 326, 328.
52 *YB* p. 337.
53 *YB* p. 357.
54 See G.W.F. Hegel, *Lectures on the Philosophy of Religion: The Consummate Religion* (ed. Peter C. Hodgson, trans. R.F. Brown and others; Berkeley; London: University of California Press, 1985), iii, 133, p. 331, pp. 330–47; G.W.H. Hegel, *Phenomenology of Spirit* (trans. A.V. Miller, analysis of text J.N. Findlay; Oxford: Clarendon Press, 1997), pp. 264–5 (440–41), 550 (440–41).
55 *GS* iii, pp. 101–9 (p. 109), cf. wf p. 254.
56 *GS* iv, p. 495.
57 *NRS* p. 305.
58 *I Knew Dietrich Bonhoeffer: Reminiscences by His Friends* (ed. Wolf-Dieter Zimmermann and Ronald Gregor Smith, trans. Käthe Gregor Smith; London: Collins, 1966), hereafter *Reminiscences*, p. 109.
59 'Commentary on Acts 2: The Founding of the Church', in *WF* p. 45; *LPP*, 'Whitsun Letter', p. 53.
60 Bonhoeffer (trans. Kelly and Nelson), in *Moral Leadership*, p. 57.
61 'Theology', *Time* 86.17 (1965): pp. 62–3, 'Is God Dead?'; *Time* 87.14 (1966): pp. 50–54 (p. 53).
62 Ralf K. Wüstenberg, 'Philosophical Influences on Bonhoeffer's "Religionless Christianity"', in *Continental Thought*, pp. 137–55, Ralf K. Wüstenberg, *Glauben als Leben: Dietrich Bonhoeffer und die nichtreligiöse Interpretation biblischer Bergriffe* (Frankfurt am Main: P. Lang, 1996), pp. 232, 342, 399. Dilthey is referred to in *LPP* pp. 187, 189, 204, 209, 227, 243, 333, 343, 377.
63 *LPP* pp. 279, 327, 342, 374, 383.
64 *LPP* pp. 381–2.
65 Wüstenberg, *Continental Thought*, p. 144.
66 *LPP* pp. 157, 240, 282, 286, 299, 329, 369, 381. For the notion of resurrection see, for example, *GS* iv, p. 454, *D* p. 114, *CF* p. 146, *WF* p. 36, *TP* pp. 48–9.
67 *LPP* pp. 336–7.

[68] *LPP* pp. 282, 336, 369–70.

[69] *LPP* p. 361.

[70] *LPP* pp. 280.

[71] LPP pp. 285–6.

[72] *LPP* p. 300.

[73] *LPP* p. 363.

[74] Trans. by Kelly, in Bethge, *Bonhoeffer*, p. 830.

[75] Zizioulas, pp. 110–11.

[76] *D* p. 287.

[77] *Spiritus Creator*, p. 3.

[78] Luther, LW, xxv, L*ectures on Romans: Glosses and Scholia* (ed. Hilton C. Oswald; St Louis: Concordia Publishing House, 1972), II, 2.15, p. 187, *Spiritus Creator*, p. 3.

[79] Luther, LW, xxxii, 'Against Latomus', *Career of the Reformer* II (ed. George W. Forell; Philadelphia: Fortress Press, 1958), p. 164.

[80] Luther, LW, xxv, VIII, 8.26, p. 365.

[81] *Spiritus Creator*, pp. 54, 303, 183.

[82] Luther, LW, xxv, I, 1.6, p. 187, I, 1.3–4, pp. 147–8, *Spiritus Creator*, p. 122.

[83] Luther, LW, xxvii, *Lectures on Galatians, 1535: Chapters 5–6, Lectures on Galatians, 1519: Chapters 1 – 6* (ed. Jaroslav Pelikan, trans. Richard Jungkuntz; St Louis: Concordia Publishing House, 1964), I, 3.2, 3, p. 249.

[84] Luther, LW, x, *First Lectures on the Psalms I, Psalms 1 – 75* (ed. Hilton C. Oswald; St Louis: Concordia Publishing House, 1974), I, Psalm 45.1, p. 212.

[85] Luther, LW, i, *Lectures on Genesis: Chapters 1 – 5* (ed. Jaroslav Pelikan; St Louis: Concordia Publishing House, 1958), I, 1.2, p. 9.

[86] See Watkin-Jones, p. 331.

Conclusion

[1] www.barackobama.com/2006/06/28/call_to_renewal_keynote_address.php (accessed 30 November 2010); see Michael, J Sandel, *Justice: What's the Right Thing To Do?* (New York: Farrar, Straus & Giroux, 2009), pp. 244–51.

[2] Justice Malala, 'SA needs visionary at the helm', *The Times*, 10 January 2011, p. 8.

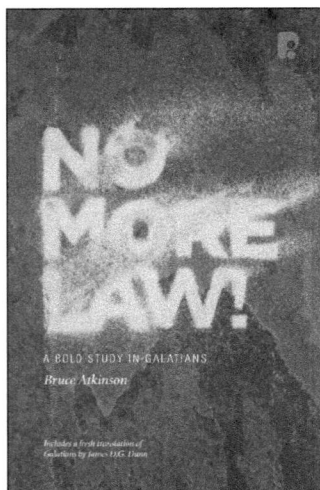

No More Law!

A Bold Study in Galatians

Bruce Atkinson

No More Law! is an accessible commentary on Paul's letter to the Galatian church. In it Bruce Atkinson concentrates on the work of the Holy Spirit in the Christian life; walking in the Spirit, how this brings freedom and produces godliness. He maintains a good theological balance between the Word and the Spirit, the gospel and the place of the Mosaic Law, freedom from that Law, but with an emphasis upon our responsibility to live godly lives in today's world.

'Bruce Atkinson offers a singularly pure treatment on the triumph of grace over law based on the book of Galatians. Powerful and convincing, his written exposition reflects his bold preaching style. *No More Law!* is first Century truth effectively applied to twenty-first Century hearts. A joy to read' – **Colin Dye, Senior Minister of Kensington Temple and a member of the National Leadership Team of the Elim Pentecostal Churches.**

Bruce Atkinson is the Associate Minister of Kensington Temple Elim Pentecostal Church, Notting Hill Gate, London.

978-1-84227-747-8

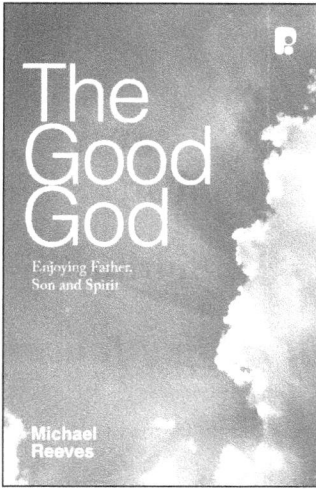

The Good God

Enjoying Father, Son and Spirit

Michael Reeves

In this lively and refreshing book, Michael Reeves unfurls the profound beauty of the Trinity, and shows how the triune God of the Bible brightens everything in a way that is happily life-changing. Prepare to enjoy the Father, Son and Spirit!

'At the heart of the universe is the passionate love between the members of the Trinity. Mike Reeves not only helps us grapple with a difficult doctrine but draws us to the magnetically attractive centre of all things. His light touch and theological wisdom combine to provide a truly helpful book which both clears your mind and warms your heart' – **Terry Virgo, Newfrontiers, UK**

'*The Good God* is a wonderful read. Reading it feels like you're eating candy floss – sweet, fun, easy. But in fact you're getting a nourishing, nutritious meal of real substance. This book will enlarge your view of God and increase love for God. You'll be blown away by the lavish love between the Father, Son and the Spirit that overflows to the world. If you want to enjoy God more then read this book – **Tim Chester, Crowded House, Sheffield, UK**

Michael Reeves is the Head of Theology for UCCF

978-1-84227-744-7

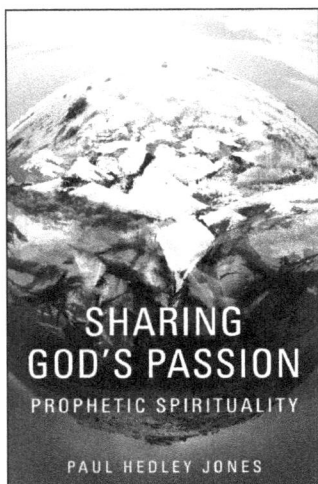

Sharing God's Passion

Prophetic Spirituality

Paul Hedley Jones

This book seeks to illuminate the critical role the prophets played in God's overarching purposes for his creation, and how we in the 21st century may also learn to collaborate with God. *Sharing God's Passion* provides a comprehensive overview of the various dimensions of a prophetic spirituality through a series of fifteen studies, each based on events in the life of the prophets, starting with Moses through to John of Patmos, including two chapters on Jesus, himself. The studies offer in-depth analyses of biblical texts, suggestions for life application, and questions for personal reflection or group discussion.

> 'Paul Jones has written a persuasive walk through the prophets. His interpretations are reliable, with an eye on the contemporaneity of these old texts. An interesting feature that commends the book is Jones's continuation of the prophetic trajectory into the New Testament' – **Walter Brueggemann, Columbia Theological Seminary**

Paul Hedley Jones is a doctoral student, working under Professor R.W.L. Moberley, at Durham University, UK.

9781842277454

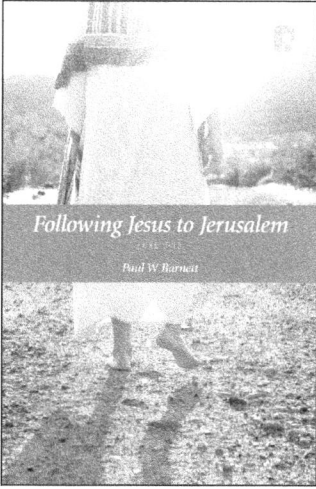

Following Jesus to Jerusalem

Luke 9–19

Paul Barnett

Taking the metaphor of life as a journey, Paul Barnett follows the journey of Jesus to Jerusalem and suggests that we journey with him. Barnett stresses the important place of kingdom in this and the ethics of Christian living which naturally follow from being in the presence of a humble saviour. More than a commentary, then, this important book challenges the way we live in the light of Jesus' last days and self-sacrifice. Paul Barnett expounds Luke, chapters 9–19, with the intention of provoking faith and faithfulness in the lives of Jesus' followers today.

Paul Barnett is the former Bishop of North Sydney and lecturer in New Testament, Moore College, Sydney, Australia

9781842277676

Paternoster:
thinking faith

We trust you enjoyed reading this book from Paternoster. If you want to be informed of any new titles from this author and other releases you can sign up to the Paternoster newsletter by contacting us:

Contact us
By Post: Paternoster
52 Presley Way
Crownhill
Milton Keynes
MK8 0ES

E-mail:paternoster@authenticmedia.co.uk

Follow us:

www.ingramcontent.com/pod-product-compliance
Lightning Source LLC
Chambersburg PA
CBHW071437090426
42737CB00011B/1687